Designing Compensation Programs for Individuals and Households After Man-Made and Natural Disasters in the United States

Steven Garber

For more information on this publication, visit www.rand.org/t/RR1005

Library of Congress Cataloging-in-Publication Data is available for this publication.
ISBN: 978-0-8330-9562-6

Published by the RAND Corporation, Santa Monica, Calif.
© Copyright 2016 RAND Corporation
RAND® is a registered trademark.

Support RAND
Make a tax-deductible charitable contribution at
www.rand.org/giving/contribute

www.rand.org

Preface

Man-made and natural disasters occur fairly frequently in the United States. Much less frequently, after a disaster occurs, ad hoc victim compensation programs (VCPs) are instituted using public and/or private funds. The designs of such VCPs—specifying who is eligible for compensation, how much compensation each person receives, procedures for claiming funds and auditing the program, and much more—have differed across programs and often engender considerable controversy. The objective of this report is to help VCP designers—the primary intended audience—make wise decisions without undue delay in compensating victims and without unnecessary administrative costs. The report does so by highlighting major issues and controversies that designers are likely to confront, considering multiple outcomes of design decisions (such as the extent of fairness, speed of compensation, and size of transaction costs), and recognizing conflicts or trade-offs in balancing such competing outcomes. Funding for this study was provided by generous philanthropic contributions to the RAND Institute for Civil Justice.

RAND Institute for Civil Justice

The RAND Institute for Civil Justice (ICJ) is dedicated to improving the civil justice system by supplying policymakers and the public with rigorous and nonpartisan research. Its studies identify trends in litigation and inform policy choices about liability, compensation, regulation, risk management, and insurance. The institute builds on a long tradition of RAND Corporation research characterized by an interdisciplinary, empirical approach to public policy issues and rigorous standards of quality, objectivity, and independence.

ICJ research is supported by pooled grants from a range of sources, including corporations, trade and professional associations, individuals, government agencies, and private foundations. All its reports are subject to peer review and disseminated widely to policymakers, practitioners in law and business, other researchers, and the public.

The ICJ is part of RAND Justice, Infrastructure, and Environment, a division of the RAND Corporation dedicated to improving policy- and decisionmaking in a wide range of policy domains, including civil and criminal justice, infrastructure protection and homeland security, transportation and energy policy, and environmental and natural resource policy.

Questions or comments about this report should be sent to the project leader, Steven Garber (Steven_Garber@rand.org). For more information about the RAND Institute for Civil Justice, see www.rand.org/icj or contact the director at icjdirector@rand.org.

Contents

Tables

Summary

Man-made and natural disasters occur fairly frequently in the United States, causing personal injury and property damage to dozens, and sometimes even thousands, of people each time. After such disasters, victim compensation programs (VCPs) are sometimes created to compensate those affected for at least some of their losses. The design of a VCP—specifying who is eligible for compensation, how much compensation each person receives, procedures for claiming funds and auditing the program, and much more—requires balancing the objectives of various stakeholders. This report offers analyses aimed at helping those who design VCPs in the United States. The focus is on monetary compensation, excluding both emergency assistance and compensation payments that public or private entities (e.g., insurers) are obligated to make for policy or contractual reasons.

The goals of this report are to help VCP designers

- anticipate issues they are likely to confront
- understand how their decisions affect victims
- consider multiple outcomes affected by their decisions
- recognize trade-offs or conflicts among these outcomes
- foresee likely sources of controversy.

To illustrate key VCP design issues, the author identifies, describes, and analyzes four governmental VCPs (GVCPs) created since 2001 and seven private VCPs (PVCPs) created since 2007. Two of the four GVCPs are federal programs compensating losses from the terrorist attacks on September 11, 2001; the other two are state-level programs involving accidents (the I-35W bridge collapse in Minneapolis and the Indiana State Fair stage collapse). Five of the seven PVCPs were responses to intentional acts—four mass shootings (Aurora, Colorado; Newtown, Connecticut; Tucson, Arizona; and Virginia Tech's campus) and an act of terrorism (the Boston Marathon bombings). Another responded to an accident (at the Reno Air Races). The seventh PVCP involved compensation for property losses from the oil spill resulting from the Deepwater Horizon oil rig explosion.

Among the 11 VCPs reviewed, there was extensive variation in the surrounding circumstances (such as the number and nature of injuries and losses) and key design decisions (such as who was eligible for compensation, the sizes of compensation payments, whether accepting compensation limited or foreclosed tort options of victims, the speed with which payments were made, and the existence of and problems caused by multiple compensation programs for the same groups of victims).

As a descriptive matter, it seems clear that the most important concern of VCP designers is being fair to victims. But there is no single, correct way to achieve that goal, because fairness means different things to different people. To illustrate issues related to fairness and their complexity, this report jointly considers three illustrative aspects of fairness: compensating on the basis of victims' needs, compensating on the basis of victims' deservingness, and maintaining horizontal equity (that is, that victims in similar circumstances should be treated similarly). Each aspect leaves considerable room for interpretation; for example, what makes a victim more or less deserving of compensation? A key practical issue in designing fair VCPs is how to operationalize abstract (and, often, not fully formed) notions within the VCP's rules. Making an operational measure of an aspect of fairness more detailed or complex will often improve fairness, but it can also negatively affect two other outcomes that typically concern VCP designers: ensuring timeliness in making compensation payments and limiting a program's transaction costs.

These outcomes often are competing and require compromises or balancing. Broadly stated, as indicators (for example, days hospitalized) become more detailed or complex to more accurately correspond to an underlying concept (for example, deservingness)—and thereby increase fairness—timeliness of payment will decline and transaction costs will increase. For instance, requiring more documentation from applicants for compensation and more-intensive auditing of claims tends to increase fairness by limiting fraudulent claiming, but it also increases administrative costs and probably delays payments. In framing compensation programs, VCP designers must balance these competing aspects and outcomes.

There is no one-size-fits-all approach or best VCP design, because the advantages and disadvantages of a design depend on the circumstances. Nevertheless, VCP designers can follow some practical suggestions to help accomplish their goals fairly, quickly, and efficiently. Such suggestions include the following:

1. Focus on the well-being of the victims of the disaster and on meeting obligations to funders and upstream VCP creators (if any) who delegate decisions to you. For example, do not concern yourself with the potential effects of your decisions on future rates of insurance uptake or self-protection efforts.

2. Recognize that eligibility decisions—which may often precede many other design decisions—are crucial. For this reason, think especially hard about eligibility rules. Your views about what is fair should provide useful guidance.

3. Be aware that assigning equal payments for all fatalities—a strategy that is inconsistent with tort principles—seems less controversial than offering unequal payments; many object on moral grounds to the idea that some lives are more valuable than others.

4. To save on administrative costs, make sure that program rules and processes are no more complex than needed to achieve other goals. For example, consider carefully whether a perhaps unfair rule would undermine fairness enough to warrant the extra delays and administrative costs that would result from implementing it.

5. Try to avoid use of donations solicited by invoking sympathy for the direct victims of the disaster to help others, such as commu-

nity members at large—such use of funds has greatly annoyed those eligible for compensation from a VCP.

6. Try to limit the number of funds or programs providing compensation to victims—ideally, to only one. Efforts to coordinate among several programs may well be futile, and they will almost surely increase payment delays and administrative costs. Thus, *preempting* the creation of multiple funds or programs seems more promising than effectively *coordinating* among them.

As mentioned, providing specific recommendations about complete designs or key features of high-quality designs seems inappropriate. For instance, the best design decisions—and the appropriateness of particular designs—can differ greatly depending on VCP-specific circumstances, such as the wishes of taxpayers or donors, the number of victims, the nature and severity of injuries, the VCP budget, and how fairness to victims is best interpreted. However, the suggestions offered here emphasize ways to improve an outcome—such as the extent of fairness, speed of compensation, and size of transaction costs—with fairly small sacrifices in other outcomes. In sum, VCP designers should carefully consider the trade-offs associated with program designs under consideration and implement VCP rules, processes, and governance to, above all else, benefit the victims.

Acknowledgments

I am indebted to several colleagues for their contributions to the report. First, I thank the two technical reviewers: Robert L. Rabin (Stanford Law School) and Nicholas M. Pace (RAND). Second, I am grateful for comments from several members of two advisory boards at RAND—namely, those of the Institute for Civil Justice and the Center for Catastrophic Risk Management and Compensation. Third, I thank Katherine Lee (RAND) for her extensive and outstanding administrative assistance. Finally, I thank Allison Kerns (RAND) for excellent editing. The author is responsible for any remaining shortcomings of the work.

Abbreviations

FEMA   Federal Emergency Management Agency

GCCF   Gulf Coast Claims Facility

GVCP   governmental victim compensation program

PVCP   private victim compensation program

VCF   victim compensation fund

VCP   victim compensation program

CHAPTER ONE

Introduction

Man-made and natural disasters raise several public and private policy issues, including compensation for losses, and such compensation is the focus of this report. *Disasters*—synonymously, *catastrophes*—are defined here as sudden events that cause large-scale damage to people or their property.[1] Natural disasters include hurricanes, floods, tornadoes, earthquakes, wildfires, and the like. Man-made disasters can be accidental (for example, airplane crashes, toxic spills, or explosions at industrial sites) or intentional (for example, terrorist acts or other acts of violence that are not politically motivated, such as arson).

In some cases, after a disaster occurs, a government or private entity decides to provide money to compensate those affected; such programs are known as victim compensation programs (VCPs).[2] Programs instituted by government entities are referred to as *governmental* VCPs (GVCPs), and programs instituted by private entities are referred to as *private* VCPs (PVCPs). The analysis in this report considers

---

[1] There is no widely accepted view on how much dollar damage or how many people must be harmed for an event to qualify as a disaster or catastrophe. Stephen D. Sugarman, for example, defines a disaster in qualitative terms: "At the society level, a disaster is generally understood as an event that causes large losses to a substantial number of people" (Sugarman, 2007, p. 1).

[2] This report does not address threshold questions concerning whether any compensation program should be instituted in response to a disaster; for example, why was a governmental program instituted to compensate victims of the terrorist attacks on September 11, 2001, but not for victims of the Oklahoma City bombing or Hurricane Katrina? For analyses of such questions, see Rabin and Sugarman, 2007; Sugarman, 2007; and Mullenix, 2014.

administrative compensation—that is, compensation through executive, rather than judicial, action—of individuals and households for personal injuries, property damage, and death.

One of the most important questions related to this topic asks how such a compensation program should be *designed*. And designing a VCP requires answering several subquestions, such as the following:

- Who should receive—or be eligible for—any compensation from the program?
- How much compensation should each eligible victim receive?
- What must claimants do to receive payments?
- How extensively will program administrators audit claims?

The purpose of this report is to help designers of VCPs make wise decisions without undue delay or administrative costs. It does so by interpreting and synthesizing scholarly and popular writing about compensation funds and developing a framework for thinking about design issues. More specifically, the goals of this report are to help VCP designers

- anticipate issues they are likely to confront
- understand how their decisions affect victims
- consider multiple outcomes affected by their decisions
- recognize trade-offs or conflicts among these outcomes
- foresee likely sources of controversy.

Scope

The analysis considers VCPs instituted and designed to respond to particular, single events that cause personal injury or property damage to numerous individuals or households. Thus, mass injuries related to product defects are within the scope of the analysis only if numerous injuries are attributable to a defect in a *single unit* of a product—for example, a defectively manufactured airliner that crashes and causes numerous fatalities or nonfatal injuries.[3] On the other hand, programs to compensate for mass injury from toxic environmental exposure are excluded, because mass injuries are not attributable to a single event. The focus here on compensation programs designed *after* or *in response to* a disaster means that the VCP is designed with that disaster and group of victims in mind. In other words, the focus in this analysis is on what others have called *ex post, ad hoc* compensation programs.[4] Finally, compensation is assumed to be in the form of cash, which is by far the most common means of compensation.[5]

Discussion

Compensation is defined here to exclude *disaster relief* or *emergency assistance*, which are provided in the immediate or short-term aftermath of a disaster to meet basic needs of victims and to prevent further

---

[3] Thus, programs to compensate victims of defects embodied in an entire product line (e.g., a particular drug, a motor vehicle model) are outside the scope of the present analysis. Such excluded compensation programs include mass-tort settlements (see, for example, Nagareda, 2007; Garber, 2013) or private compensation offered as an alternative to tort, such as the recent General Motors program related to ignition switches (Bronstad, 2015).

[4] Authors have distinguished between *ex ante* and *ex post* compensation programs (see, for example, Faure and Hartlief, 2006; Faure, 2007). There are several ex ante compensation programs in the United States—that is, programs created and designed before the relevant injuries occur. Examples of ex ante schedules of compensation include state workers' compensation programs and the federal program to compensate those injured by selected vaccines.

[5] As Feinberg (2012) points out, "in deciding who gets what in American society, money is almost always the vehicle of exchange" (p. 186), and "when we discuss how to compensate innocent victims of wrongdoing . . . Americans rely on money" (p. 187). However, there are examples of noncash compensation; for example, the Federal Emergency Management Agency (FEMA) has provided temporary housing in the form of trailers, and the University of Connecticut's Newtown Scholarship Fund ("UConn Scholarship Fund for Sandy Hook Survivors Raises $1M," 2013), to which more than 5,000 people have donated, provides scholarships. The emphasis in this report on cash compensation reflects the emphasis on cash in practice.

damage to people and property.[6] In contrast, compensation, which is usually provided after an emergency ends, is intended to increase the well-being of victims or their survivors by paying for some of the losses resulting from the disaster.

The compensation relevant to the present analysis also excludes payments that governments or private entities are obligated to make by law or contract. Both governments and private entities enter into contracts with individuals and households to cover some of the kinds of losses considered here. For example, in addition to offering health and life insurance policies, many private insurers write homeowners' and renters' insurance policies covering property damage from hurricanes, fires, and earthquakes. Moreover, the federal government and some state governments sell insurance covering specific kinds of disasters. More specifically, the federal government insures property losses caused by flooding under the National Flood Insurance Program,[7] California provides insurance for earthquake damage through the California Earthquake Authority,[8] and Florida (as an insurer of last resort) provides property insurance that includes wind coverage.[9]

Organization of This Report

Chapter Two describes relationships between VCPs and the tort system, providing background for the analysis. Chapter Three describes four GVCPs, and Chapter Four considers seven PVCPs by tabulating their key features and then comparing and contrasting several aspects of

---

[6] FEMA often provides disaster relief as authorized by the Stafford Act (Rabin and Bratis, 2006, pp. 312–319; Bea, 2010). This relief includes, for example, short-term unemployment compensation and assistance with short-term expenses, such as costs of temporary housing. This assistance is not intended to provide compensation for losses by individuals or households (in contrast to public entities, which are often compensated through FEMA for infrastructure damage).

[7] See, for example, Rabin and Bratis, 2006, pp. 312–322; and Dixon et al., 2006, pp. 51–56.

[8] See, for example, Rabin and Bratis, 2006, pp. 327–330; and LaTourette et al., 2010.

[9] See, for example, Citizens Property Insurance Corporation, 2014; Jametti and von Ungern-Sternberg, 2011; and Rabin and Bratis, 2006, p. 349.

such programs. Chapter Five categorizes the types of decisions that VCP designers face, organizing them in terms of rules, processes, and governance. Chapter Six outlines the goals of VCP designers and identifies conflicts or trade-offs among them. Finally, Chapter Seven offers suggestions for VCP designers and provides concluding remarks.

Victim Compensation Programs and the Tort System

Depending on the context, administrative compensation can supplement or substitute for compensation through the tort system. Sometimes, avoiding litigation is an express goal of establishing a compensation program, as was the case with the September 11th Victim Compensation Fund of 2001 (see Chapter Three). However, compensation through the tort system is sometimes impossible because the losses result from "acts of God" (as with natural disasters),[1] those responsible for accidents cannot be identified or are judgment-proof, or those who intentionally cause disasters (such as terrorists and arsonists) are dead or judgment-proof.

The U.S. government and many state governments are protected from tort liability based on the doctrine of "sovereign immunity," but public entities can be held liable in tort in some circumstances. Many states have waived some of this protection, although at least 33 of them have instituted caps on the amount of damages for which they can be liable (Findley, 2013).[2]

Often, designers of VCPs have to decide whether acceptance of compensation affects victims' ability to pursue tort claims, and if so, how. More specifically, designers of GVCPs may choose to foreclose or limit tort actions by victims. And while designers of PVCPs generally do not have the legal authority to directly foreclose or limit tort actions

---

[1] Tort suits alleging failure to mitigate losses before—for example, by properly designing and constructing dams—or after the catastrophic event can be viable, however.

[2] For information about state law on sovereign immunity and tort claims, see National Conference of State Legislatures, 2010.

by victims, they can (and sometimes do) make receipt of compensation funds conditional on waiving tort rights. Moreover, when tort claims are legally viable and not foreclosed as a condition for receiving compensation from a victim compensation fund (VCF), such compensation may be viewed as a "collateral" source in tort and thereby reduce damages available from tort actions.

The doctrines and processes of the U.S. tort system can substantially influence the designs of both governmental and private compensation programs.[3] For example, those who design VCPs may be greatly influenced by instincts or intuition about justice or fairness that derive, in large measure, from those designers' experiences with tort principles and processes. For example, when the number of victims is fairly large, as with mass torts, determinations of losses and compensation payments for each victim based on their detailed, individual circumstances can be impractical because of the required delays and administrative expenses. Accordingly, the processes for settling mass torts—for which individualized justice is impractical for the same reasons—can greatly influence the design of a compensation program. More specifically, a VCP may be designed to assign victims to different groups or categories, and all victims within each category receive the same amount of compensation. Alternatively, compensation levels may be determined by formulas involving measures of or surrogates for the nature and severity of the injuries suffered by each victim.

---

[3]   See the discussion later in this report about the guiding principles of a VCP, which are often framed in terms of whether a compensation program should be more like tort or more like public social-welfare programs.

CHAPTER THREE

Governmental Victim Compensation Programs

Since 2001, public or private entities in the United States instituted at least 11 *ex post, ad hoc* VCPs that provided compensation to individuals or households for personal injuries and/or property damage. This chapter and Chapter Four describe these 11 programs.

These descriptions are not comprehensive case studies; in fact, the amount of publicly available information about the programs varies, from fairly limited to very extensive. Moreover, because a single individual (Kenneth R. Feinberg) designed and administered most of the programs and advised designers of others,[1] it is likely that these histories involve less variety in design decisions than would otherwise have been the case. The descriptions offered here do, however, serve the purposes for which they were developed—namely, to provide context, background, and examples for the analyses that follow.

Four GVCPs are described in this chapter, including two programs resulting from the terrorist attacks on September 11, 2001 (9/11), which are the only two federal GVCPs instituted in the United States in recent history.[2] For clarity and expositional convenience, this report refers to these GVCPs as the 9/11 VCF of 2001 and the 9/11 VCF of 2011. Next, we turn to the state-level GVCPs, including one created in

---

[1] See Table 4.1 in Chapter Four.

[2] While the 9/11 VCF is widely described as unprecedented, publicly funded compensation predates the terrorist attacks on September 11 (Landis, 1998). For example, the United States instituted a compensation program for damage caused by the British during the War of 1812 (Landis, 1998; Dauber, 2003).

the aftermath of a bridge collapse in Minneapolis and one created after a stage collapse at the Indiana State Fair.

PVCPs, and the remaining seven VCP examples, are described in Chapter Four.

The 9/11 VCF of 2001

The September 11th Victim Compensation Fund provided compensation to people who were injured and to survivors of those killed by the terrorist attacks.[3] The fund was created by Congress only 11 days after those attacks.[4]

To receive compensation from the fund, victims were required to waive their rights to sue in tort; those rights had been curtailed—but not eliminated—by the legislation that created the fund (the Air Transportation Safety and System Stabilization Act). Congress required that victims should be compensated for their economic (such as lost income) and, more controversially, noneconomic (such as pain and suffering) losses and that compensation from other (collateral) sources would be deducted from amounts of compensation otherwise available from the fund. These requirements are key elements of tort doctrine, and as the primary designer of the fund writes, "The tort system and the 9/11 fund were joined at the hip" (Feinberg, 2012, p. 59).

A particularly controversial implication of compensating economic losses as they would be compensated in tort, which many

---

[3] Mullenix and Stewart (2002–2003) and Stewart, Cohen, and Marangi (2002–2003) compare features of the 9/11 VCF with those of other governmental compensation programs, such as the National Swine Flu Act of 1976, National Childhood Vaccine Injury Act of 1986, Black Lung Benefits Act, Radiation Exposure Compensation Act of 1990, Energy Employees Occupational Illness Compensation Program Act of 2000, and Price-Anderson Act of 1957. None of these programs, however, is an *ex post* response to a specific and sudden catastrophic event; thus, none is an example of a VCP as defined in this report.

[4] There are many accounts of this compensation program, and the account in this text relies on the following sources: Feinberg, 2005, 2011/2012, Chapter 2; Feinberg et al., 2004; Mullenix and Stewart, 2002–2003; Stewart, Cohen, and Marangi, 2002–2003; and selected articles from Vol. 53 of the *DePaul Law Review*, including Alexander, 2003; Dauber, 2003; Diller, 2003; Katz, 2003; Peck, 2003; and Priest, 2003.

viewed as unfair, was that fatalities of high earners were compensated at higher levels (Feinberg, 2005, pp. 34–37; Feinberg, 2012, p. 63). Moreover, the requirement that compensation received from collateral sources be deducted from compensation amounts available from the fund (so-called "offsets" for collateral sources) became very problematic in the context of compensation from charitable donations. When push came to shove, compensation payments from charities were not offset in determining payments from the public fund (Feinberg, 2005, pp. 70–71).

Congress also directed that compensation payments would be tax free and that there would be no judicial review or congressional oversight of decisions made by the fund's special master. Finally, Congress placed no limit on the amount of money that could be paid out by the fund.[5]

The remaining design decisions were delegated to a special master, and the U.S. attorney general appointed Kenneth R. Feinberg to this position. In total, the program paid out about $7 billion to roughly 5,500 claimants. Mean awards for fatalities were a little more than $2 million, and median awards were a little less than $1.7 million.

Many commentators and legal scholars have criticized the rules and implementation of the 9/11 VCF of 2001. Such critiques emphasize such issues as reliance on an uneasy mixture (or hybrid) of compensation principles from tort, insurance, and social welfare; limited transparency; the extensive discretion by the fund's special master; and the absence of appeal mechanisms.[6]

---

[5] The availability of unlimited funds would greatly simplify matters for the VCP designers. For example, in discussing the 9/11 VCF of 2001, Peck (2003, p. 220) states that once the Price-Anderson Act was chosen to serve as the general framework, the "only two issues" in designing the fund were "eligibility and the amount of damages suffered."

[6] See, for example, Rabin, 2001; Alexander, 2003; Diller, 2003; Priest, 2003; Berkowitz, 2006; Rabin and Sugarman, 2007; and Mullenix, 2011.

The 9/11 VCF of 2011

The second federal GVCP—instituted by the James Zadroga 9/11 Health and Compensation Act of 2010—is technically a reactivation of the earlier 9/11 VCF of 2001.[7] This compensation program was reauthorized for an additional five years on December 18, 2015. This fund offers compensation for physical injury to people who, as a direct result of the September 11, 2001, attacks, were killed, are suffering traumatic injury, or have selected health conditions (judged to be causally related); who participated in removal of debris from any of the three sites; or who were otherwise exposed to the debris. Unlike the 9/11 VCF of 2001—which focused on fatalities and nonfatal injuries caused by trauma—the 9/11 VCF of 2011 provides compensation for injuries related to possibly long-delayed illnesses (such as cancers) and deaths caused by toxic exposures. In relation to the traumatic fatal and nonfatal injuries addressed by the original fund, then, the 9/11 VCF of 2011 raises difficult issues involving injury causation, as well as the potential for compensable injuries becoming manifest only after the program expires or the funds are exhausted.

As with the 9/11 VCF of 2001, decisions of the program's special master (Sheila L. Birnbaum) cannot be appealed in the courts (Birnbaum, 2013). Unlike the 9/11 VCF of 2001, however, this program has a limited budget. The 2010 legislation provided $2.775 billion to cover compensation payments and administrative costs, and the 2015 reauthorization provided an additional $4.6 billion. At the time of this writing (spring 2016), the fund administrators were revising procedures to comply with requirements from the reauthorization. The remainder of this description of the 9/11 VCF of 2011 focuses on the situation prior to the 2015 reauthorization.

The 2010 Zadroga Act limited payments during the first five years of the program to $875 million, with final payments to have been made in year six (2016). As with the 9/11 VCF of 2001, payments from a wide array of collateral sources are to be deducted from (or used

---

[7]   This account is based on September 11th Victim Compensation Fund, undated, 2015; and U.S. Department of Justice, 2011.

to offset) compensation awards, and accepting compensation requires waiving rights to sue in tort. As a step toward setting final compensation levels that will be feasible given the program's limited budget, the program administrators determine levels of compensation for eligible claimants—based on the federal legislation and tort principles—that would be appropriate if funds were unlimited. If the total of these full compensation levels exceeds the program budget, however, awards will be scaled back proportionately so that there is enough money to go around.

As of September 6, 2015, the program had received 20,622 eligibility forms; of these, 12,150 had been approved, and 6,285 decisions about full compensation levels had been made.

I-35W Bridge Collapse in Minneapolis

On August 1, 2007, a bridge over the Mississippi River on the westbound side of Interstate 35 (I-35W) in Minneapolis, Minnesota, collapsed, causing 13 deaths and roughly 145 injuries.[8] Minnesota law limits tort damages against the state to $400,000 per person, with an aggregate limit of $1 million per event. In the case of this bridge collapse, however, these limits were exceeded. Specifically, the Minnesota legislature passed special legislation and provided almost $40 million for an *ex ante, ad hoc* GVCP. To receive compensation through the program, recipients were required to waive their rights to sue the state, its municipalities, and their employees, but accepting money from the fund did not preclude tort actions against private parties. VCP design decisions not determined by the legislation were delegated to a panel of three special masters. The state reached settlements with all 179 eligible victims, for a total of roughly $36.5 million in compensation funds.

---

[8] This account is based on Steenson and Sayler, 2009; Henson, 2009; and Minneapolis Foundation, 2009.

Indiana State Fair Stage Collapse

On August 13, 2011, a performance stage at the Indiana State Fair collapsed,[9] causing seven fatalities and more than 50 nonfatal injuries.[10] At least one potential private tort defendant had participated in designing a compensation program that required waiver of tort rights, but when it became apparent that the program would not nearly end litigation against that defendant, it withdrew from that effort.

Administrative compensation totaling $11 million was paid out by the state of Indiana in two phases. First, $5 million—the maximum liability of the state under the Indiana Tort Claims Act—was paid out to cover settlements reached in December 2011 with 62 victims. In this first phase, the estates of those killed were offered $300,000 each, and those who were not fatally injured were offered 65 percent of their medical expenses to date (thereby not taking future medical costs into account). All but one of these settlement offers were accepted. In the second phase, an additional $6 million was paid out to the settling victims as authorized by an act of the Indiana legislature (the House Enrolled Act 1376) in March 2012, which brought total compensation for each fatality to $700,000, the maximum available to a single victim under the Indiana Tort Claims Act. Total compensation payments for nonfatal (physical) injuries ranged from less than $500 to more than $1.1 million.

In addition to this GVCP, there was also a PVCP for the victims, funded through charitable donations.[11] More specifically, on August 15, 2011 (two days after the incident), the Central Indiana Community Foundation established the Indiana State Fair Remembrance Fund to accept private donations, and these donations, along with other private contributions, financed the Indiana State Relief

---

[9]   Much of this account is based on Office of the Indiana Attorney General, 2012, 2014; Campbell, 2012; Findley, 2013; Associated Press, 2015; Disis, 2014; and Stafford, 2012, 2014.

[10]   Different sources report different numbers of nonfatal injuries; the number reported most often by the most reputable sources was 57.

[11]   This paragraph is based on information reported in Indiana State Fair Commission, undated, 2011; and "Last of State Fair Relief Fund Distributed to Victims Monday," 2011.

Fund, which was designed and administered by Kenneth R. Feinberg. The fund provided $35,000 for each death claim. For nonfatal injury claims, the amount of compensation depended on numbers of days and nights the victim was hospitalized—specifically, $25,000 for ten or more days and nights of hospitalization, $7,500 for between four and nine days and nights, or $3,000 for between one and three days and nights. Those who were injured but not hospitalized were not eligible for compensation from this PVCP.[12]

For a description of a recent disaster that resulted in government compensation but no distinct VCP, see the box below.

Governmental Compensation Without a Distinct VCP: Hurricane Sandy

There is no federal GVCP (as defined here) for victims of Hurricane Sandy, which caused massive damage in Connecticut, New Jersey, and New York on October 29, 2012. Nonetheless, it is instructive for the purposes of this report to recognize that federal money has been used to compensate some of the property losses of individuals and households. Considering Hurricane Sandy illustrates and highlights two key points. First, compensation of the kinds considered in this report can be—and sometimes is—provided without establishing a formal VCP. Second, when there is no such VCP, it can be especially difficult to document compensation patterns and characterize the implicit design of the compensation activities.

Federal money provided to state and local entities in the areas affected by Hurricane Sandy is being used to compensate some individuals for property losses and to repair homes. More specifically, some of the $60.2 billion appropriated by Congress in January 2013 to support recovery from the storm will be used to repair or knock down buildings, including homes, damaged by the storm. For example, New York City is using $648 million in federal funds to buy or to help repair or rebuild residential properties ("Stronger Than the Storm—Hurricane Sandy One Year On," 2013), and New Jersey plans to use some of its federal money to rebuild or demolish houses (Parry, 2013). Despite the lack of freestanding, formal GVCPs, such efforts require many of the same program-design decisions discussed in this report.

As of late August 2014—almost two years after the storm—New York City's "Build It Back" program was beginning to develop some momentum, but, at most, 1,000 victims had received money or started repairs under the program. The state programs in New York and New Jersey seem to have made considerably more progress, with reimbursements to more than 7,000 homeowners in New York, totaling $350 million, and with 3,800 New Jersey homeowners having signed agreements involving about $450 million (Kusisto, 2014).

---

[12] Moreover, victims of the stage collapse reached settlements with 18 private defendants for a total of $39 million; how the settlement was to be distributed among the victims was confidential (Stafford, 2014).

CHAPTER FOUR

Private Victim Compensation Programs

This chapter considers seven PVCPs since 2007, detailing their known design features in a table and then comparing and contrasting those features.

Table 4.1 provides overviews of seven PVCPs set up in response to man-made disasters since 2007.[1] The table describes the disasters and provides information about what appear to be the most important (and prominent) PVCPs resulting from these disasters.[2] For most of these disasters, there were multiple compensation funds; however, there is little information to be found about funds not listed in the table.

---

[1] *Ex post, ad hoc* PVCPs responding to particular natural disasters appear to be rare. The Revere [Massachusetts] Tornado Relief Fund, a PVCP established in response to a tornado in 2014, provided more than $250,000 in compensation to roughly 150 claimants (City of Revere, 2014). In addition, the Napa Valley Community Disaster Relief Fund provided money for local residents and businesses in the aftermath of the earthquake in the Napa Valley in August 2014, established with a lead gift of $10 million from Napa Valley Vintners. Much, and perhaps all, of the money for residents was earmarked for disaster assistance, including "repairs for immediate safety concerns" (Napa Valley Vintners, undated).

[2] The main sources used to develop the information in Table 4.1 and related discussion in this chapter are as follows: (1) for the Aurora theater shooting, Brumfeld, 2012; and Deam, 2013; (2) for the Boston Marathon bombing, Bernstein, 2013a, 2013b; Abel, 2014; and Fox, 2104; (3) for the Deepwater Horizon oil spill, Feinberg, 2012, Chapter 6; and McDonell, 2012; (4) for the Reno airplane crash, Reno Air Races Accident Compensation Program, undated; and "$77 Million Fund Created for Reno Air Races Crash Victims," 2012; (5) for the Newtown school shooting, Applebome, 2013; Associated Press, 2013a, 2013b; Christoffersen, 2013; Deam, 2013; Newtown–Sandy Hook Community Foundation, 2013; State of Connecticut, 2013; and Altimari, 2014; (6) for the Tucson shooting, Burbank, undated; and (7) for the Virginia Tech campus shooting, Virginia Tech, Office of University Relations, 2007; and Feinberg, 2012, Chapter 4.

Table 4.1
Overview of Seven Private Victim Compensation Programs Since 2007

Incident	Victims	Fund Name and History	Compensation Payments, Other Uses of Funds	Selected Rules for Eligibility
Aurora, Colo. Shooting at movie theater, July 20, 2012	12 fatalities, 70 others injured	• Aurora Victim Relief Fund, established July 23, 2012, by Community First Foundation at the request of the governor; • Special Master: Kenneth R. Feinberg	• Total = $5.34 million, paid out by mid-November 2012 • $220,000 to the family of each deceased victim (n = 12) • $160,000 for being hospitalized 20+ days (n = 6) • $91,680 for being hospitalized 8–19 days (n = 2) • $35,000 for being hospitalized 1–7 days (n = 13) • 57 claims, 38 approved	• No compensation unless hospitalized (due to limited funds)
Boston Marathon, Mass. Bombing near finish line, April 15, 2013	4 fatalities, 256 others injured	• One Fund Boston, Inc., established one day after the incident • Special Master: Kenneth R. Feinberg	• Total = $60.9 million awarded to 232 victims, June 2013 ○ $2.195 million to double amputees and to families of those killed (n = 6) ○ $1.2 million to single amputees (n = 14) ○ $948,000 for being hospitalized 32+ nights (n = 10) ○ $125,000 for being hospitalized 1–2 nights (n = 18) ○ $8,000 for being treated at the hospital but not admitted (n = 143) • A second distribution of $18.5 million awarded summer 2014 (more than a year after the bombing)	• Do not have to relinquish tort rights to accept an award • May also collect from other funds established for individuals or small groups • Psychological injuries not covered

Table 4.1—Continued

Incident	Victims	Fund Name and History	Compensation Payments, Other Uses of Funds	Selected Rules for Eligibility
Deepwater Horizon, Gulf of Mexico Oil spill from oil rig explosion, April 20, 2010	11 fatalities on the rig, almost all other damage was to property and business	• Gulf Coast Claims Facility (GCCF) • Administrator: Kenneth R. Feinberg	• $20 billion fund to compensate all victims (individuals and businesses), as well as natural resource damages • BP allowed to sue other parties, such as Transocean and Halliburton. As of March 9, 2012 (two years after the explosion): ○ 1.06 million claims filed; ○ 0.42 million claims denied ○ 169,000 claims paid, totaling $6.14 billion	Phase 1: • 90-day emergency payments, no waiver of right to sue Phase 2: Eligible claimants choose one of the following: • *quick* payment—if a claimant had received an emergency payment, $5,000 for individuals and $25,000 for businesses, and the claimant must waive tort rights • *interim* payment— document ongoing damage quarterly; no waiver of tort rights • *final* payment: document past and future losses; waive rights to sue and to return to GCCF

Table 4.1—Continued

Incident	Victims	Fund Name and History	Compensation Payments, Other Uses of Funds	Selected Rules for Eligibility
National Championship Air Races, Reno, Nev. Plane crashes into crowd, September 16, 2011	11 fatalities, (including pilot), at least 70 serious injuries	• Reno Air Racing Association Compensation Fund, established August 2012 (almost 1 year after the crash) • About $77 million available to compensate; claiming deadline October 5, 2012 • Administrator: Kenneth R. Feinberg	• Compensation for documented out-of-pocket economic losses (e.g., medical expenses, lost income) • Injury compensation (in addition to economic losses): $15,000, $45,000, and $75,000 for "minimal," "moderate," and "major" injuries, respectively • Fatalities and noneconomic damages (pain and suffering) compensated based on a point system, with dollar value of points to be determined after all claims processed	• Claimants waive their right to pursue litigation for damages caused by the crash • Appeals allowed to the fund administrator only

Table 4.1—Continued

Incident	Victims	Fund Name and History	Compensation Payments, Other Uses of Funds	Selected Rules for Eligibility
Sandy Hook Elementary School, Newtown, Conn. Shooting, December 14, 2012	26 fatalities (20 children and 6 educators); 12 1st graders who were in the classroom survived, 2 teachers injured	• United Way and Newtown Savings Bank created Sandy Hook School Support Fund and then turned over $11 million to Newtown–Sandy Hook Community Foundation (NSHCF); final plan released mid-July 2013 • Administered by Review Board of volunteers from the community (Kenneth R. Feinberg provided advice) • Other funds: My Sandy Hook Fund; Sandy Hook Promise (compensation and gun violence advocacy)	• $7.7 million paid to 40 victims or families: ○ $281,000 to each family of the deceased (n = 26) ○ $75,000 to victims of physical injury (n = 2) ○ $20,000 to children present in the classroom (n = 12) • My Sandy Hook Fund raised $1.5 million, distributed equally to the families of the 26 fatalities (about $58,000 per family)	• The fund reserved about $4.3 million to support community needs related to the shooting • Appeals allowed to Review Board only

Table 4.1—Continued

Incident	Victims	Fund Name and History	Compensation Payments, Other Uses of Funds	Selected Rules for Eligibility

Tucson, Ariz. Shooting, January 8, 2011	6 fatalities, 13 wounded	• Tucson Together Fund formed by merger of three funds, and received donations totaling about $520,000
		 • Fund was shut down on February 14, 2013 (about 2 years after the shooting)
		 • Kenneth R. Feinberg was asked for and offered advice
			• Total compensation funds equaled $470,000
			 • The fund paid out two rounds of $5,000 compensation payments, totaling $185,000
			 • Maximum payouts from the fund for expenses:
			   o deceased next of kin: $25,000
			   o survivor who was shot: $20,000
			   o witness or victim who was not shot: $5,000
				• Examples of expenses eligible for reimbursement: lost wages, funeral expenses, travel, counseling
				 • $50,000 set aside for future claimants

Virginia Tech, Blacksburg, Va. Shooting, April 16, 2007	32 fatalities, including 27 students and 5 faculty	• Hokie Spirit Memorial Fund, set up to distribute private contributions
		 • Administrator: Kenneth R. Feinberg
			• $6.5 million, distributed the last week of October 2007:
			   o $208,000 for families of the deceased (n = 32)
			   o $90,000 and tuition and fee waiver if hospitalized 10+ days and nights
			   o $40,000 and tuition and fee waiver if hospitalized 3–9 days
			   o $10,000 or tuition and fee waiver if hospitalized fewer than 3 days
			   o $10,000 or tuition and fee waiver to those in specific classrooms and not covered above through physical injury (for mental trauma)
				• Recipients free to sue the university
				 • Contributions from donors specifying "scholarship fund" were used for that purpose

Causes of Injury

Five of the seven disasters resulting in PVCPs were intentional. Four of them involved mass shootings—at a movie theater in Aurora, Colorado; Sandy Hook Elementary School in Newtown, Connecticut; a political event in Tucson, Arizona; and the campus of Virginia Tech (Virginia Polytechnic Institute and State University) in Blacksburg, Virginia. The fifth, the Boston Marathon bombing, was an act of terrorism. The funding for these five compensation programs came from donations to long-established charities and to new entities created in response to the particular disasters.

The other two PVCPs summarized in Table 4.1 resulted from accidents—namely, the explosion of the Deepwater Horizon oil rig and subsequent oil spill in the Gulf of Mexico and an airplane that crashed into the crowd at the Reno Air Races.

The Deepwater Horizon event is the only one of the seven disasters for which the losses were primarily economic—rather than personal injury—and for which businesses, in addition to individuals, could receive compensation. Because there were multiple potential tort defendants that were identifiable and had deep pockets, the GCCF can be viewed as part of an effort to resolve a mass tort. Critiques of the GCCF—such as Mullenix (2011), Partlett and Weaver (2011), and Conk (2012)—have raised concerns pertaining to its fairness and effectiveness as a compensation program and as a potential model for resolving future mass tort claims. Mullenix (2011, p. 823), for example, writes, "The GCCF has raised challenging ethical and professional responsibility issues, as well as questions relating to the fund's transparency."

Budgets

The ability of a PVCP to provide compensation is limited by its budget. Total amounts paid in compensation from the seven PVCPs summarized in Table 4.1 vary significantly, from less than $0.5 million (Tucson), to several million (Aurora, Sandy Hook, Virginia Tech), to tens of millions (Boston Marathon, Reno Air Races)—all of which were funded by charitable donations—to several billion dollars (Deepwater Horizon), which was funded by BP.

Eligibility for Compensation

The last column of Table 4.1 describes selected rules for eligibility for payment. Some involve exclusion of some types of injury; for example, Aurora victims who were not hospitalized and Boston Marathon victims with only psychological injuries were ineligible for payments. Moreover, physically injured Boston victims who were not hospitalized all received the same payments, apparently "in the interest of distributing the money quickly" (Bernstein, 2013a). In the aftermath of the Virginia Tech shooting, to cover mental trauma, the Hokie Spirit Memorial Fund offered compensation (in cash or waivers of tuition and fees) to people who were not physically injured but were in classrooms where shooting occurred. Despite its modest budget, the Tucson program opted for fairly broad eligibility by providing compensation to witnesses of the shooting who were not physically injured.

Sizes of Compensation Payments

Some have argued for "equality" or "uniformity" of compensation levels in compensation programs, especially for fatalities (Diller, 2003, p. 728; Feinberg, 2012, pp. 183–185; Mullenix, 2014).[3] As reported in the table, however, compensation levels differ across eligible, surviving victims in the seven PVCPs, as well as in the four GVCPs discussed in Chapter Three. But in six of the private programs (excepting the GCCF for the Gulf Coast oil spill), compensation for fatalities was the same among each disaster's eligible claimants, although the sizes of those

---

[3] Feinberg argues for uniformity of compensation payments across victims in the context of future GVCPs in response to terrorism losses, writing that uniformity would "minimize claimant divisiveness . . . [and] provide a streamlined process for speedy payment of claims" (2005, pp. 183–185).

payments differed across disasters, depending on the amount of money available per victim. Specifically, payments for fatalities varied widely: For Tucson victims, such payments were $25,000 (there were six fatalities, and the fund had less than $500,000 to distribute); in the cases of Aurora, Sandy Hook, and Virginia Tech, payments ranged between $200,000 and $300,000; and for the Boston Marathon bombing, payments exceeded $2.2 million.

The six PVCPs besides the Gulf Coast fund provided different compensation levels for nonfatal injuries by using multiple categories that were defined in terms of surrogates for severity of injury. These surrogates—which are fairly simple and easy to verify—include number of days hospitalized (Aurora, Boston Marathon, Virginia Tech) or nature of injury (Sandy Hook, Tucson). As with fatality policies, none of the programs provided for different payment levels based on the income or wealth of victims or their families, however.

Timing of Payments

Program designers typically consider it desirable to make compensation payments quickly—for example, because doing so benefits the victims whom the program is designed to help. As reported in Table 4.1, the Boston Marathon bombing and Aurora shooting PVCPs provided compensation payments within four and five months of these events, respectively, and payments were distributed from the Hokie Spirit Memorial Fund less than seven months after the Virginia Tech shooting.

Uncertain Budgets and Future Claims

Two impediments to quick payment from a VCP are uncertainty about the eventual budget (especially while fundraising is still ongoing) and uncertainty about the number and nature of future claims or victim needs. Different VCPs have used different procedures to respond to this uncertainty. First, payments can be made in stages ("interim" payments), as was done in the PVCPs for the victims of the Boston Marathon bombing and the Tucson shootings (as well as the 9/11 VCF of 2011, as required by the 2010 Zadroga legislation).[4] Second, money can be set aside for future claimants, as was done in the case of the Tucson shooting. Third, point systems can be used—as in the program for the Reno Air Races crash—to enable evaluation of claims without a final determination of how points will eventually translate into compensation dollars.[5]

Rights to Pursue Litigation

Some of the seven PVCPs described in this report required recipients of compensation to waive their rights to pursue tort litigation (some Deepwater Horizon victims, Reno Air Races), and other programs did not require such waivers (Boston Marathon, Virginia Tech, some Deepwater Horizon victims). Based on available information, it is unclear whether the remaining PVCPs required waiving tort rights.

Multiple Compensation Funds

For many—and perhaps all—of the disasters described in this report, compensation was paid to victims outside of the main VCPs highlighted here. For example, in the aftermath of the Sandy Hook Elementary School shooting in Newtown, Connecticut, 77 organizations raised more than $28 million (Altimari, 2014). Furthermore, in addition to payments from the public GVCP, victims of the September 11 terror-

---

[4] In the case of the Aurora shootings, late in August 2012 (roughly a month after the incident), the Colorado Organization of Victim Assistance—rather than the Aurora Victim Relief Fund—provided $5,000 to each of the 70 families with members killed or injured (Deam, 2012a). The Colorado Organization of Victim Assistance is a "nonprofit statewide membership organization, with over 800 members throughout Colorado" (Colorado Organization of Victim Assistance, undated).

[5] Point systems have been used to settle mass tort claims, such as with Merck's now-discontinued drug, Vioxx; see, for example, Garber, 2013, pp. 32–35.

ist attacks in New York City alone received more than $2.7 billion in compensation from charitable organizations (Dixon and Stern, 2004, pp. 138–140).

The existence of multiple sources of compensation can greatly complicate the tasks of VCP designers and impede them from achieving their goals. First, for VCP designers who seek to distribute their funds to promote fairness among victims, compensation payments from other sources can result in total compensation levels for each victim that are inconsistent with the designers' equity goals. Second, when a victim receives other compensation from charitable sources and VCP designers decide to deduct that amount from the payment from their programs, they are likely to find that the associated administrative costs are uncomfortably high; they are also likely to encounter stiff resistance from charitable organizations, as was the case for the 9/11 VCP of 2001 (see Feinberg, 2005, pp. 70–71).

In sum, the existence of multiple sources of compensation can be problematic by affecting the fairness of compensation from all sources combined, and attempts to coordinate compensation across different funds can require large administrative expenses, can delay payments to victims, and might even be futile. Perhaps the best approach to avoiding such difficulties is to take quick action to prevent the emergence of multiple funds. This was the approach successfully adopted in response to the Boston Marathon bombings. More specifically, by the day after the bombing—thanks to the foresight and leadership of Boston's mayor, Massachusetts's governor, and business leaders—the One Fund Boston was created to receive donations and distribute them to victims (Deam, 2013).

Use of Charitable Donations

Some of the disasters that led to the creation of PVCPs involved major controversies about how charitable organizations used the donations they received (Deam, 2013). In particular, some traditional charitable organizations and private foundations raised money to help themselves respond to a particular disaster, but rather than using all of the donations to compensate people who were injured or who lost loved ones, the organizations used at least some of the donations to support community needs related to the disaster. Such use of donations became a major controversy surrounding compensation of victims of the Aurora (Alcindor and Dorell, 2012), Virginia Tech (Deam, 2013), and Sandy Hook shootings (Ly, 2013; Altimari, 2013, 2014; Weizel, 2014). Avoiding such controversies was another motivation for quickly establishing the One Fund Boston to receive donations and use all of the money to compensate victims of the Boston Marathon bombings (Deam, 2013).

CHAPTER FIVE

Design Decisions

The design of a VCP involves many features and, thus, many decisions. Among these decisions is the program's budget—the total amount of money available to pay claims and cover administrative costs. Designing a VCP when funds are limited is much more challenging than when funds are unlimited. Thus, the discussion that follows focuses on situations with limited funds,[1] and it is assumed that available funds do not suffice to enable fully compensating all losses from the disaster, as full compensation is widely interpreted in the context of tort litigation. Much of what follows is nonetheless relevant to situations in which available funds are unlimited.

Constrained by their budgets, program designers determine

- guiding principles
- procedures for making design decisions
- who is eligible for compensation
- how much eligible claimants should receive
- claiming processes
- deadlines.

The following classification scheme divides design decisions into three sets of decisions: rules, processes, and governance.

---

[1] The 9/11 VCF of 2001 seems to be the sole exception to limited funds, although the $20 billion budget of the GCCF related to the oil spill might be viewed as effectively unlimited.

Rules

A VCP's *rules* include, first and foremost, who is eligible for any compensation and the formulas determining the amounts of compensation to be paid to each eligible victim. These payout formulas may be simple—for example, every eligible victim is to receive the same amount of money—or complex. A complex payout formula might take the form of a table (or "grid" or "matrix") specifying payout amounts depending on such factors as (surrogates for) the nature and severity of the loss experienced by each victim. None of the seven PVCPs described in Chapter Four involves equal payment to all victims; Table 4.1 also provides several examples of how payment amounts might depend on the nature and severity of injuries.

Processes

A VCP's *processes* pertain to the actions that are taken by a VCP's administrators and claimants. For example, one such process might involve notifying the public of proposed or preliminary rules, receiving comments, and considering such comments in finalizing the rules. In the case of a federal GVCP, this is the formal rulemaking process required under the federal Administrative Procedure Act—that is, publishing a notice of proposed rules in the *Federal Register* calling for public comment, considering comments, and finalizing the rules. Both of the September 11 GVCPs went through this formal process. There may or may not be an analogous process for a PVCP; designers of private programs might, for example, invite comments from victims, the donors providing the PVCP's funds, members of the community affected by the disaster, or even the public at large.[2]

Other processes for any VCP pertain to making a claim for compensation. These processes specify what information and documentation claimants must provide to receive compensation, as well as what

---

[2]   Of course, PVCP designers are likely to receive such comments even if they do not invite them.

deadlines they must meet. Designers must also develop forms for claimants to use to apply for compensation. In addition, claiming processes include the steps taken by or on behalf of the VCP's administrators to audit or verify the completeness and accuracy of information submitted.

Governance

The *governance* of a VCP pertains to the roles of actors other than program designers, administrators, and claimants in the design and implementation of the program. For example, are the processes and rules of the program subject to appeal? If appeals are allowed, what issues may be appealed, with whom must appeals be lodged, how must appeals be made, and by when? And what rules and procedures govern the adjudication of appeals?[3]

A second central aspect of VCP governance is the *transparency* with which the decisions of program designers and administrators do their work. For example, transparency was considered to be imperative by the special master of the 9/11 VCF of 2001 (Feinberg, 2005). Moreover, in the context of GVCPs, the American Bar Association stated, "Principles of equal treatment, due process, and transparency should govern the distribution of compensation and disaster assistance" (American Bar Association, 2007, p. 7).

---

[3] Kuppa-Apte (2011) reports that Feinberg prefers having oversight, because giving unchecked power to program administrators is worrisome.

CHAPTER SIX

Major Goals of VCP Designers

Often, there are two distinct sets of actors whose decisions determine a VCP's design. Members of the first set—who might be thought of as the program "creators"—typically determine the program budget. They may also articulate the fundamental purposes or goals of the VCP and more-tangible design features, such as maximum or minimum compensation levels. These actors then typically delegate program implementation and the remaining program design decisions to others, whom we refer to as the "program administrators" or "special masters."

Consider, first, the two sets of actors who craft a federal GVCP. The first set (the "creator") is the U.S. Congress, and the second set is the person, group of people, or organization to which Congress delegates remaining design decisions—conforming to the guidance or constraints that Congress specified when creating the program. In the context of PVCPs, the first type of actor, but not the second type, is fundamentally different from its analog for GVCPs. In particular, in the case of private programs, the actors who determine the budget and specify guiding principles and constraints are not public officials acting in their public capacities. Rather, they are those who either raised the money to fund the program or are empowered by those actors.

Three broad outcomes of concern to VCP designers are apparent from what designers and onlookers emphasize—namely, the extent of fairness, speed of compensation, and size of transaction costs. As we will see, there are conflicts or trade-offs in jointly pursuing these outcomes. More specifically, in many instances, one outcome can be improved only by accepting worse outcomes in terms of one or both of the others. Presumably, designers wish to strike an appropriate balance among the three broad outcomes. Further complicating VCP design is the fact that there are multiple dimensions or aspects of fairness, among which there are also conflicts.

Major Goal 1: Being Fair

Fairness to Victims

Fairness to victims figures prominently in discussions of VCPs generally and of particular programs, for at least two reasons.[1] First, program designers want to be fair. Second, victims, their advocates, and policy advocates typically raise fairness arguments about a program's design both before and after the design is finalized. Thus, concerns about fairness in determining eligibility for and amounts of compensation and other matters are central as a program is designed.[2] For example, in the context of the 9/11 VCF of 2001, Feinberg (2005, p. 44) writes that "fair procedures . . . were essential." Fair outcomes are also a central concern.

Assessing fairness requires value judgments that differ substantially among reasonable, well-meaning participants in VCPs, as well as onlookers and commentators. On that score, Mullenix (2014, p. 31) writes, "there are many philosophical approaches to concepts of distributive justice, each of which might compel a different compensation scheme." Moreover, Feinberg (2005, p. 72) observed that "the ethical

---

[1]   The central role of fairness concerns in the design of VCPs is indicated by the title of a book by Feinberg, the special master of the 9/11 VCF of 2001 and special master or administrator of five of the seven funds described in Table 4.1; the title of that book is *Who Gets What—Fair Compensation After Tragedy and Financial Upheaval* (Feinberg, 2012). Furthermore, Feinberg (2005, p. 157) has stated that he tried to "make certain that rich and poor alike received their fair share according to the statute."

[2]   There are lessons to be learned about what advocates will assert is "fair" from the histories of compensation programs discussed in Feinberg, 2005, 2012; Abel, 2014; Alcindor and Dorell, 2012; Altimari, 2014; Bernstein, 2103b, 2013c; and Deam, 2012a, 2012b, 2013.

and philosophical issues aren't as clear-cut as they might appear to a grieving family."

This report highlights and discusses three broad aspects of fairness to victims that are seemingly invoked—explicitly or implicitly—in most discussions of VCPs. These aspects are *need*, *deservingness*, and *horizontal equity*. As will become apparent, conceptualizing and applying notions of fairness leave lots of room for discretion, even for program designers who choose to focus on these three aspects of fairness.

Social Welfare or Tort?

A helpful perspective on the distinction between need and deservingness is often raised in the context of the 9/11 VCP of 2001. The question is whether a particular VCP is—or should be—more like tort or more like social welfare. This is a question about the guiding principles of the program. Diller (2003) reports that social welfare programs typically focus on need, while there is no role for need under tort doctrine.[3] Diller (2003, p. 728) argues that GVCPs should focus on need, equality of treatment, and administrative efficiency. Thus, it may be very helpful for program designers to consider whether the purpose of the program being designed is more like social welfare or more like tort. In the context of the 9/11 VCF of 2001, Rabin and Bratis (2006, p. 339) describe tort as addressing how "deserving" a victim is and contrast this concept with that of need. These authors also refer to the proper roles of need versus deservingness as reflecting a "fundamental philosophical difference" (2006, p. 339).

Need

Need for compensation pertains to the financial circumstances in which victims or their survivors will find themselves with different amounts of cash compensation, including none at all. But—like *fairness*—*need* means different things to different people. For example, in the context of the 9/11 VCF of 2001, Feinberg (2005, p. 151) writes that, by

---

[3] More specifically, Diller (2003, p. 725) writes, "the social welfare system focuses on meeting needs, and emphasizes the values of parity between claimants and administrative efficiency, while the tort system seeks to replace losses and stresses individualized consideration of each claim."

specifying that financial hardship should be considered in determining compensation amounts, "Congress virtually guaranteed a heated economic and philosophical debate revolving around the meaning and scope of 'need.'"

A widespread view is that people with less money have greater need—and thus should (other things being equal) receive more compensation. Despite major differences across social welfare programs, features of particular programs may provide additional guidance for VCP designers hoping to operationalize the need levels of victims.[4]

Operational indicators of need. Abstract, philosophical concepts of need can take VCP designers only so far; the designers must also translate the concepts into operational measures or indicators to use in a program's rules and processes. Table 6.1 presents examples of alternative indicators of need (as well as deservingness and horizontal equity). Such indicators reflect different interpretations of need—involving different levels of complexity—that VCP administrators could measure.

The simplest indicator of need listed in the table is a claimant's total loss from the disaster. This measure, however, is a fairly crude indicator of need; for example, using this measure would, in effect, implicitly assume that a wealthy household that suffers $100,000 in damage would be equally as needy as a low-wealth household suffering the same amount of damage. This shortcoming could be addressed, however, by using the two indicators listed next in the table: total loss relative to income or to wealth. And while wealth is a more precise indicator of need than income is, income is likely to be easier for claimants to document and program administrators to verify. The first three indicators, however, ignore sources of compensation other than the VCP being designed. In principle, victims have less need (other things being equal) the more they collect from other compensation sources, such as insurers, charities, or other VCPs instituted to respond to the same disaster.

Program designers might consider additional factors in choosing operational indicators of victims' needs. For example, in the context

---

[4]　See, for example, Stewart, Cohen, and Marangi, 2002–2003; and Mullenix and Stewart, 2002–2003.

Table 6.1
Aspects of Fairness to Victims: Concepts and Implementation

Aspect	Concepts and Value Judgments	Operational Indicators
Need	Concept: Victims have more need the lower their standards of living without compensation from the VCP. Value judgment: Other things being equal, victims with greater need should be favored in designing VCPs.	Alternative measures of need: 1. total loss from disaster 2. total loss relative to income 3. total loss relative to wealth 4. (1), (2), or (3) adjusted for payments from other sources.
Deservingness	Concept: Victims are more deserving if they did more to protect themselves from financial and/or physical losses. Value judgment: Other things being equal, more-deserving victims should be favored in designing VCPs.	Alternative measures of degrees of self-protection: A. Financial self-protection/insurance: 1. any insurance? 2. insurance coverage relative to the maximum available 3. required insurance premium(s) as a percentage of income 4. (2) and/or (3) adjusted for availability of insurance. B. Physical self-protection (natural disasters): 1. located people and property in a low-risk area? 2. fortified property against relevant disaster type?
Horizontal equity	Concept: Victims in identical or similar circumstances should be treated identically or similarly. Value judgment: People in identical or similar situations should be treated similarly in designing VCPs.	Alternative measures of degrees of personal injury: A. Fatalities 1. all deaths alike 2. distinguish deaths by (for example) age or pain and suffering. B. Nonfatal injuries 1. all injuries alike 2. multiple categories of injury based on days hospitalized 3. multiple categories of injury based on pain and suffering, future medical expenses, and so on.

of property losses, designers might consider whether damage to such goods as fine art and expensive automobiles should be compensated at all or, if they are, whether there should be limits on compensation for damage to such items. Feinberg (2005, p. 152) writes that, in his role as special master of the 9/11 VCF of 2011, he "refused to subsidize extravagant lifestyles" and suggested that multiple cars, tuition to private schools, and summer homes might be considered extravagant.

Deservingness

Deservingness of compensation is distinct from *need* for compensation. One view of deservingness involves the compensation amounts that victims merit because of how their actions affected their precompensation losses. A seemingly common perspective on deservingness focuses on what victims did to protect or endanger themselves—financially or physically—before the disaster occurred.[5] For example, buying insurance is a form of financial self-protection, whereas victims who put themselves or their property in harm's way—for example, in flood plains, near coastlines prone to hurricanes, near known major earthquake fault lines, or in areas unusually susceptible to wildfires—exemplify physical self-endangerment.[6] Along these lines, many accept the basic principle that victims are more deserving of compensation (other things being equal) if they did more to protect themselves from damage and less deserving if they knowingly put themselves or their property

---

[5] The VCP in the aftermath of the Deepwater Horizon explosion and oil spill suggests a perspective on deservingness that does not involve self-protection. Rather, it pertains to the ethics of claimants' behavior that is not directly related to the disaster and could be relevant whenever victims' losses include lost income. Specifically, in the context of the GCCF, claimants who could not document lost income—often, it seems, because they did not keep records or file tax returns—wound up with relatively small compensation payments. Reduction of compensation payments to victims unable to document lost income for such reasons is likely to result from VCP processes and claim forms that require documentation of lost income. Going beyond the example of working off the books, other unethical or illegal behavior could be deemed relevant to VCP designers. For example, compensation might be denied to someone who negligently caused a wildfire.

[6] Physical self-protection is much more pertinent to natural than man-made disasters. For example, most victims of terrorist acts or mass shootings cannot be viewed as knowingly putting themselves in harm's way.

in harm's way.[7] When determining eligibility and amounts of compensation, many VCP designers are likely to conclude that whether and how insurance purchases should be taken into account depends on the availability of disaster-relevant kinds of insurance at reasonable or affordable premiums.[8] However, there are no established criteria for determining whether insurance premiums are "reasonable" or "affordable."[9]

The idea that self-protection should be a major consideration in gauging deservingness is implicit in a principle proposed by the American Bar Association. Specifically, the organization suggests that a policy worthy of consideration is "reduction in government compensation that is made available to persons affected by a major disaster for those affected persons who decline, without sufficient cause, available insurance coverage or undertake unreasonable risks with respect to exposure to major disasters" (American Bar Association, 2007, p. 6).

Operational indicators of deservingness. As is the case for operationalizing the concept of need, VCP designers who want to take deservingness into account must develop measurable indicators of deservingness, and there are several plausible choices. Table 6.1 offers examples based on linking deservingness to self-protective behavior before a disaster.

Financial self-protection could involve insurance against damage from specific risks, such as floods and earthquakes, or against types of losses covered for a variety of causes, such as homeowners' or renters'

---

[7] The "knowingly" qualification is made to avoid the implication that, for example, victims of school shootings are less deserving because they put themselves in harm's way. Such victims could not know that they were in harm's way, whereas people who live on the Atlantic coast in Florida, for example, might reasonably know that they are at risk of being harmed by a hurricane.

[8] In determining the amount of federal assistance a victim may receive for property damage, FEMA must consider (among other things) whether insurance was "reasonably available." To make this determination, FEMA "relies on the assessments of [the] state insurance commissioner" (Rabin and Bratis, 2006, p. 320).

[9] For example, many homeowners who are required to purchase insurance from the National Flood Insurance Program do not comply with this requirement (Dixon et al., 2006); therefore, designers of a VCP responding to a flood might deem such homeowners to be undeserving of compensation or deduct from their compensation payments the amount that flood insurance would have paid.

insurance for property damage or health or life insurance for personal injury. The simplest plausible indicator—and the first listed for deservingness in Table 6.1—might be whether a victim had any insurance relevant to the losses caused by the disaster. This indicator might be too crude for VCP designers to embrace, however, because the higher the maximum coverage purchased, then the higher the degree of self-protection. The second illustrative indicator responds to this fact by expressing the amount of insurance purchased (e.g., the coverage limit minus the deductible) as a proportion of the maximum amount that could have been purchased. Further complicating matters is a widespread view that lack of insurance or fairly small levels of coverage should not disadvantage victims in the eyes of a VCP designer if insurance premiums were too high to be reasonable or affordable. The third indicator in Table 6.1 reflects concerns about affordability by suggesting that VCP rules relevant to deservingness should operationalize self-protection in terms of the required premium (for maximum coverage, for example) relative to income. The fourth and final illustrative indicator is even more complicated than the others; it involves adjusting the second or third indicator of deservingness to account for how reasonable insurance premiums were.

Physical self-protection seems relevant to natural disasters, but rarely, if ever, to man-made disasters. In the context of natural disasters, self-protection can—as suggested by the two indicators listed in the table—involve both where victims chose to locate themselves and their property and, given these locations, whether property was fortified.

Horizontal Equity

In discussing fairness, economists often distinguish between vertical and horizontal equity. In the context of VCPs, vertical equity requires that eligibility and relative compensation levels for victims in different circumstances should reflect their relative levels of, for example, need, deservingness, or some combination of the two. Concerns about vertical equity, then, are implicit in how designers use assessments of different victims' needs and deservingness to determine eligibility and compensation levels.

In contrast to vertical equity, *horizontal equity* refers to the comparative treatment of people in identical or (more practically) similar circumstances. In the context of VCPs, horizontal equity suggests that those who experienced similar losses should all be either eligible or ineligible for compensation and, if eligible, should receive similar compensation payments.

Developing practical implications of horizontal equity, building them into VCP designs, and implementing them are hardly straightforward. Several complications are apparent. Most fundamentally, it is not clear which characteristics of victims or their losses are the most appropriate (fair) focuses for gauging similarity. In designing and implementing the 9/11 VCF of 2001, special master Feinberg found the horizontal equity principle appealing in theory but unhelpful in practice. In particular, he writes, "I tried to treat similar claims alike. But I soon learned there were few truly 'similar' claims" (Feinberg, 2005, p. 89). Moreover, reflecting on his experience as special master of the 9/11 VCF of 2001, he stated that "if Congress decides to provide compensation in the event of a new terrorist attack, all eligible claimants should receive the same amount" for "numerous practical reasons" Feinberg (2005, p. 183).[10]

Operational indicators of horizontal equity. As with policies considering need and deservingness, VCP designers who are concerned about horizontal equity must translate abstract notions—in this case "identical or similar circumstances"—into operational indicators. Table 6.1 suggests alternative measures in the context of personal injury, first for fatalities and then for nonfatal injuries.

The first, and simplest, listed indicator for fatalities would treat all fatalities alike. This is the approach taken in six of the PVCPs described in Table 4.1 (all but the GCCF for the Gulf Coast oil spill), as well as in the GVCP following the stage collapse at the Indiana State Fair. However, VCP designers might not compensate all fatalities with the same amount of money, as in the two GVCPs responding to the terror-

---

[10] Such reasons include a desire to limit divisiveness among victims, the time required to determine economic losses on an individualized basis, and challenges in determining what compensation claimants have received from other (collateral) sources.

ist attacks on September 11, 2001, for which compensation amounts are based on tort principles. The second indicator in Table 6.1 accounts for such principles by suggesting that it might be fairer (as in the case of tort) to provide higher payments to younger victims (because more years of life were lost) or for deaths involving more pain and suffering.

For nonfatal injuries, the first illustrative indicator of horizontal equity would treat all injuries (that exceed a severity threshold that must be determined) alike. However, none of the PVCPs from Chapter Four treated all nonfatal injuries in the same way, and all of those programs used somewhat crude surrogates for injury severity. The second listed indicator, then, distinguishes among nonfatal injuries on the basis of numbers of days hospitalized—as was done in the PVCPs for the Boston Marathon bombing and the shootings in Aurora and Virginia Tech. Injuries might be divided into categories of severity. Of course, the potential degree of horizontal equity will be greater the more categories that are used and the better those categories reflect respected value judgments about what factors make victims more and less alike for the purposes of VCP design. The third listed indicator would refine the second indicator by considering—in addition to days hospitalized—pain and suffering, future medical expenses, and so on.

Conflicts Among Aspects of Fairness

We have seen that, when determining fair rules for eligibility and fair amounts of compensation, designers confront substantial challenges, including choosing aspects of fairness (such as need, deservingness, and horizontal equity) for focus, developing abstract characterizations of those aspects, and choosing operational measures or indicators to use to determine eligibility and compensation levels.

Further complicating matters for VCP designers who seek to accommodate more than one aspect of fairness, many design decisions that improve one aspect of fairness will worsen other aspects. For example, designers must consider how to treat compensation that victims receive from sources outside the VCP being designed—that is, collateral sources.[11] Such sources include payouts from life insur-

---

[11] For a brief discussion of the collateral source rule in tort, see Rabin and Bratis, 2006, p. 353.

ance for fatalities; health insurance for personal injuries; homeowners', renters', earthquake, and flood insurance for property damage; other VCPs established to compensate victims of the same disaster; charitable donations made directly to victims; and proceeds from litigation (when VCP rules do not require waiving all tort rights).

In the context of insurance payments, a conflict arises between need and deservingness. More specifically, deducting insurance payouts in determining eligibility or compensation amounts tends to give more weight to need than to deservingness,[12] because money that victims receive from insurance decreases their need, but buying insurance is a form of self-protection that many would say increases deservingness.

Summing Up

Designing a VCP to treat victims fairly is very challenging for several reasons. First, and most fundamentally, fairness means different things to different people. Thus, program designers should expect to be criticized or challenged on fairness grounds no matter what they do. Second, fairness is multidimensional—this chapter has focused on need, deservingness, and horizontal equity—and, as just discussed, there can be conflicting implications of increasing fairness in different dimensions. Third, operationalizing abstract principles or notions of fairness requires considerable thought, not only about what is fair but also about conflicts or trade-offs between fairness and other major concerns of program designers. More specifically, as discussed later in this chapter, the speed of compensation payments often declines and program administrative costs often increase when more-refined operational indicators of fairness are adopted.

Fairness to Nonvictims

While most of the concern about fairness in designing VCPs centers on being fair to victims, VCP designers may also have substantial concerns about being fair to nonvictims, such as the taxpayers and donors

---

[12] Feinberg (2005, p. 185) recommends that collateral sources not be deducted, at least for future GVCPs in the wake of terrorist attacks.

who fund GVCPs and PVCPs, respectively. To the extent that funders want victims to be treated fairly, VCP designers can be fairer to funders by being fairer to victims.

Fraudulent claiming in compensation programs has received considerable attention from VCP designers, as well as onlookers. Fraud works against achieving all three aspects of fairness discussed above and, it seems, any other aspect of fairness that VCP designers are likely to embrace. More specifically, excess compensation payments that result from misrepresentation reduce the precision with which a VCP respects need, deservingness, and horizontal equity. Moreover, avoiding payment of fraudulent claims might also be viewed as promoting fairness to taxpayers and donors who do not want their money to go to people who break the program's rules.

Both of the GVCPs resulting from the terrorist attacks on September 11 include extensive steps to deter and detect fraudulent claims. In the 9/11 VCF of 2001, claimants were required to document their losses, and potential instances of fraud were referred to the Justice Department.[13] Moreover, the claim forms for compensation from the fund included language designed to deter fraud by informing claimants about potential legal penalties for providing false information.[14] Similarly, for the 9/11 VCF of 2011, the eligibility claim form attempts to deter fraud by citing potential legal penalties.[15]

---

[13] Feinberg (2005, p. 87) writes, "I tried to protect the fund from fraudulent claims by requiring detailed documentation and by asking the Department of Justice Fraud Division to investigate any suspicious claims that came our way." There were 26 such claims, and six people were prosecuted and convicted.

[14] The claim forms included the following statement: "You must certify that the information contained in and attached to the Compensation Form is true and accurate. The Special Master will apply various procedures to verify, authenticate, and audit claims. False statements may result in fines, imprisonment, and/or any other remedy available by law. The Special Master shall refer all evidence of false or fraudulent claims to the Department of Justice and other appropriate law enforcement authorities" (Feinberg et al., 2004, exhibits C and D).

[15] The eligibility form instructions state, "You must certify under penalty of perjury that all information contained in and submitted with the Eligibility and Compensation Forms is true and accurate. False statements or claims made in connection with this application may result in fines, imprisonment and/or any other remedy available by law to the federal government" (September 11th Victim Compensation Fund, 2013, p. 3).

Deterrence of fraudulent claiming can be fortified in other ways. For example, VCP program administrators and other relevant actors can facilitate media coverage of the arrest and punishment of violators to enhance general deterrence. At least 15 people were indicted for fraudulent claims with the GCCF (Barnett, 2010), at least three people have been arrested for fraudulent claims to the One Fund Boston (Annear, 2013; Landers, 2013; Andersen, 2013), and at least two have been arrested in connection with the Indiana State Fair VCP (CNN Wire Staff, 2011).

Major Goal 2: Ensuring Timely Compensation

While fairness is a central—and sometimes, the paramount—concern of VCP designers, at least two other concerns are evident in the design of VCPs: the timeliness with which compensation payments are made and the transaction costs involved in designing and operating VCPs.

Designers of VCPs are concerned about how quickly compensation payments are made, especially because unnecessary delays can increase the suffering of victims. For example, some victims may be unable to pay their bills or restore their property while waiting for compensation, and receipt of payments can help some victims put memories of traumatic events behind them. Delays in paying claims were a major complaint of some victims of the Aurora shootings (Deam, 2012a).

The timeliness with which compensation payments are made depends on how long it takes for VCP designers and administrators to proceed through several steps, each of which can take more or less time depending on the program's design. Such steps include obtaining the money required for the VCP, making design decisions, receiving and processing claims, making payments, and dealing with appeals. But program designers need not complete each step before starting the next. For example, some design decisions can be made before all funds have been raised, although administrators cannot determine final payment levels without knowing how much money will eventually be available. In addition, claiming can commence as soon as claim forms are developed and before the total amount of available money is determined. Claim processing, including auditing, also can commence as soon as any claims are received and before the deadline for filing claims. Furthermore, payouts can commence before all claims are submitted and processed.

Major Goal 3: Limiting Transaction Costs

Program designers want to limit the transaction costs involved in designing and administering VCPs. These costs include the salaries and wages paid to program designers, administrators, claims processors, and auditors; travel expenses; and costs associated with creating websites, developing claim and other forms, disseminating information to the public, and so on. As these transaction costs increase, the money available for compensation payments decreases, at least for a VCP with a limited budget. An exception is the VCP created for victims of the Tucson shooting, in which funds were raised with a promise that all money would go to the victims, and the Pima County Attorney's Office paid expenses related to the Tucson Together Fund, including the creation of a website, the initial donation processing costs, and salaries of staff to administer the fund (Burbank, undated, p. 2).

Transaction costs also include victims' time, aggravation, and inconvenience in pursuing their claims within the VCP. The category can also include victims' out-of-pocket expenses, such as legal fees when a victim chooses to consult a lawyer about accepting compensation payments from a VCP, which may require waiving rights to pursue litigation.[16] While such costs receive relatively little attention in discussions about VCPs, program designers should try to limit these costs in

---

[16] More than 1,100 lawyers provided free legal services to potential claimants from the 9/11 VCF of 2001 (Stewart, Cohen, and Marangi, 2002–2003, p. 160; Peck, 2003, p. 225; Trial Lawyers Care, undated). This free advice benefited victims by shifting transaction costs from them to participating lawyers. The Zadroga Act, which created the 9/11 VCF of 2011, capped lawyers' fees at 10 percent of the compensation payment obtained (U.S. Department of Justice, 2011, p. 54117).

the interest of helping victims. Moreover, more onerous demands on victims can undermine fairness by discouraging them to file claims.[17]

Conflicts Among Being Fair, Ensuring Timely Compensation, and Limiting Transaction Costs

There are clear conflicts or trade-offs in trying to achieve fairness, ensure timeliness of compensation, and limit a program's transaction costs. As emphasized earlier in this chapter, the more refined or nuanced a VCP's definition of fairness is, the less contentious and more legitimate the program is perceived to be. However, as a result of that refined definition, the operational measures or indicators of fairness are more complicated. And more-refined program rules often lead to more required documentation, more to audit, additional delays in compensation, and higher transactions costs. In another example of conflicts among these competing outcomes, enforcement of program rules is viewed by many to be crucial to fairness, but more-extensive auditing of applications for compensation increases transactions costs and likely delays processing claims and remitting payments.

Activities that increase transaction costs may, however, be crucial to addressing other policy concerns. For example, requiring more-extensive documentation of eligibility for compensation and more-frequent and detailed auditing of claims tends to reduce the incidence of payments to those who are not eligible, thereby promoting fairness. But (again) requiring such documentation and auditing also increases the transaction costs borne by both the program and claimants and likely delays filing claims, processing claims, and remitting payments.

---

[17] For example, Feinberg (2005, p. 44) writes, "if the claim form itself were too consumer unfriendly, applicants would be reluctant to apply."

Effects of VCP Design on Future Losses

At least in theory, the design of a VCP can affect the levels of uncompensated losses to households from future natural events, disastrous or not. This can occur by affecting the extent of both financial and physical self-protective behavior of potential victims. For example, if people expect that the government will compensate them for damages suffered during a hurricane, they might feel more comfortable buying a house on the Florida coast and not purchasing insurance. There is little indication that VCP designers care about potential long-term effects of their design decisions, and unless the guiding principles they receive from the creators of the programs include this, why should they care? Nonetheless, some commentators call attention to these issues and assert that this should concern VCP designers, which seems to make more sense for GVCPs than for PVCPs.

A fundamental insight linking provision of compensation for losses to self-protective behavior is that, at least in theory, anticipated future availability of other sources of compensation attenuates the incentives for homeowners and other individuals to protect themselves—and the more generous such compensation is expected to be, the stronger this effect. This idea has figured prominently in many discussions of appropriate public policies in response to man-made and natural catastrophes—see, for example, Epstein (1996), Harrington (2000), and Conrad and Thomas (2013), all of which argue that governmental compensation should be avoided because of its adverse effects on self-protection.

The theory supporting this insight relies on assumptions employed in economists' simplest models of decisionmaking in the face of risk.[18] Such models, however, ignore considerations that are viewed as fundamental by many researchers and lead to predictions that conflict with

---

[18] For example, these models typically rely on an assumption that prospective victims maximize their expected utility levels by relying on knowledge of the true probability of experiencing losses of various magnitudes.

experimental evidence and observed patterns of behavior in real-world settings.[19]

Financial Self-Protection

As the uptake and coverage levels of relevant kinds of insurance rise, the extent of uncompensated losses from future disasters shrinks, other things being equal. Moreover, in its sixth principle, the American Bar Association (2007, p. 6) expresses a preference for relying on insurance: "To the fullest extent permitted by law the persons affected by a major disaster should be compensated for their losses through insurance coverage and the operation of the judicial system."

Many accept the view that VCPs can reduce insurance uptake, and the more generous that VCPs are, the greater this effect will be. There are, however, many reasons to question the existence or importance of such effects. For example, there are several reasons to doubt that demand for insurance is usefully represented by any simple economic model. Reasons for this include lack of affordability of insurance for many households, misjudgment of and inability to work with probabilities (such as simply ignoring low-probability events), unfounded beliefs that "it will not happen to me," and the tendency of some households to perceive insurance as an investment and then cancel coverage after a few years if the investment has not paid off.

Physical Self-Protection

There are two fundamental ways that homeowners could reduce the physical damage to their property and the risks of personal injury or death caused by a natural event of a given severity in a given location. First, homeowners could locate their properties in areas less prone to damage from natural events. Second, they could increase the ability of their properties to withstand damage (often called *mitigation*). As is the case with financial self-protection, VCPs can, in theory, reduce physi-

---

[19] For more discussion of these issues in the context of demand for insurance, see Faure, 2007, pp. 346–347. For discussion in the contexts of demand for insurance and loss-mitigating behavior, see Wharton Risk Management and Decision Processes Center, 2008, Chapters 5 and 12.

cal self-protective behavior, and the more generous that VCPs are, the greater this effect will be. However, simple economic theories predict patterns of behavior that are greatly at odds with empirical evidence.

CHAPTER SEVEN

Suggestions for VCP Designers

The primary aim of this concluding chapter is to provide practical suggestions for VCP designers. Recommendations that apply to major decisions for all, or even most, VCPs cannot be developed for several reasons, such as fundamental (and unresolvable) disagreements about the meaning of fairness, differences across disasters in the number and nature of injuries, differences in budgets across VCPs, and extensive uncertainty about such key issues as how much compensation victims have received or will receive from other sources. In short, when it comes to designing VCPs, one size cannot fit all.

The chapter is organized as follows: First, there is a brief recap of major points from the previous chapters. The next section discusses interests that tend to either divide or unite victims. The subsequent section discusses how a VCP designer might best help victims while satisfying the designer's obligations to the program's funders. The next section offers several suggestions for how VCP designers can help victims, and the last section offers brief summary remarks.

Recap

This report considers the design of VCPs—created after man-made and natural disasters—for individuals and households suffering personal injury and property losses. The focus is on monetary compensation, excluding both emergency assistance and compensation payments that public or private entities (e.g., insurers) are obligated to make for policy or contractual reasons.

Designers of VCPs face daunting challenges for several reasons, including the numerous reasonable views about the meaning and design implications of fairness, disparate circumstances and concerns among victims, multiple stakeholders with conflicting views, and the effects of design decisions on multiple outcomes. The outcomes of leading concern to VCP designers appear to be the extent of fairness, speed of compensation, and size of transaction costs.

As discussed in the analysis, these outcomes often are competing and require compromises or balancing. Broadly stated, as indicators become more detailed or complex to more accurately correspond to an underlying aspect of fairness—and thereby tend to increase fairness—timeliness of payment will decline and transaction costs will increase. For example, requiring more documentation from applicants for compensation and more-intensive auditing of claims tends to increase fairness by limiting fraudulent claiming, but it also increases administrative costs and probably delays payments. In framing compensation programs, VCP designers must balance these competing aspects and outcomes.

Victims Have Conflicting and Shared Interests

VCP designers cannot make all victims happy—even with an unlimited budget. But they may be able to avoid or mitigate controversies that threaten a program's ability to do the best it can for victims jointly.

Relative Compensation Levels Tend to Divide Victims

The leading cause of dissension among victims appears to be how the total compensation payments are distributed. This seems to be the case even when the available funds suffice to provide *all* victims with payments that many would view as very generous. In reflecting on his experience as the administrator of the 9/11 VCF of 2001, the Hokie Spirit Memorial Fund, and the GCCF, Feinberg states that establishing a VCP in response to a disaster creates "a sense of entitlement" among its victims and that "everyone counts other people's money" (Feinberg, 2012, p. 189). Moreover, "The problem is also exacerbated when there are only finite dollars to distribute" (Feinberg, 2012, p. 190). But this behavior seems not to be specific to VCPs that have fairly small budgets and thus small compensation levels. In particular, Feinberg indicates that such envy and counting of other people's money characterized even the 9/11 VCF of 2001, which had an unlimited budget and provided much higher levels of compensation than most, if not all, other VCPs.

Thus, we can expect that victims will be unhappy about VCP rules and processes that tend to decrease their compensation relative to that of other victims. Some VCP rules can pit different subgroups of victims against each other. These include rules about (1) compensation levels for fatalities relative to nonfatal injuries of different kinds and severity and (2) collateral source offsets for insurance payouts or compensation received directly from charities or other VCPs. Moreover, rules about who is eligible for *any* compensation are all or nothing, so arguably appropriate compensation candidates who believe that they are entitled to compensation but get none at all can become greatly disgruntled. In sum, as Feinberg (2005, pp. 189–190) writes, "'Rough justice' in establishing these compensation programs—the pursuit of the greatest good for the greatest number—means very little to each individual expecting fair treatment from the administrator or special master."

Maximizing Total Compensation Tends to Unite Victims

There are several outcomes of VCP designs that tend to unite those who are eligible for compensation. First and foremost, victims who are deemed eligible want the total compensation pool that will be divided among them to be as large as possible. Some requirements for maximizing "the size of the pie" are deterring fraudulent claims in least-cost ways and limiting administrative costs that come out of the VCP's total budget.

Other goals that tend to unite eligible claimants include making compensation payments quickly, limiting paperwork burdens on claimants, and preventing fundraising that suggests that it will help direct victims but whose funds actually will be used for other purposes, such as helping the community at large.

How Can Designers Best Help Victims?

Because helping victims is the primary goal of VCPs, designers have obligations to those victims. Moreover, explicitly or implicitly, designers may have obligations to those who provide a VCP's funds—namely, taxpayers and donors—and to those who created the VCP and delegated remaining design decisions (for example, to a special master). How these obligations are best balanced across the three groups requires value judgments, and reasonable people are likely to disagree about such judgments.

There are many ways to conceptualize how VCP designers might best go about balancing the desires of victims, funders, and VCP creators. A respectable—and relatively simple—posture for VCP designers is that they should try to maximize benefits, as a whole, to the victims while fulfilling their obligations to the other two groups. For convenience in exposition, let us assume that VCP designers adopt this posture (even though "fulfilling obligations" leaves considerable room for interpretation).

Maximizing "benefits, as a whole, to the victims" involves more than maximizing the total amount of compensation payments. Most victims care about more than the sizes of their compensation payments, and, thus, their well-being depends on more than how much money they receive. First, most victims care about how long they have to wait to receive compensation payments. However, the importance of speed is likely to differ greatly among eligible victims; for example, some victims can comfortably pay their bills before receiving their compensation payments. Second, victims would like to minimize their burdens in filing and documenting their own claims for compensation. As with speed of compensation, the size of transaction costs borne by victims is likely to differ substantially—depending, for example, on whether they find it easy or hard to understand the claim forms and collect the required documentation. Third, many victims are likely to resent—and be aggravated to varying degrees by—fundraising that appeals to their plight when a substantial portion of the resulting donations will be used to benefit nonvictims.

VCP designers face huge challenges. Despite enormous uncertainty about the preferences of victims and funders, for example, VCP designers are expected to accomplish the following: maximize victim benefits as a whole, which requires effort to increase the size of the pool of money available to compensate; speed up payments; limit administrative and other transaction costs; deter fraudulent claiming; and respect the wishes of funders, among other things. Moreover, when the number of victims is fairly large—say, several dozen or more—it can be impractical to consider every victim's case individually in much detail, because doing so likely requires unacceptable delays and involves unacceptably high administrative costs.

What's a VCP Designer to Do?

The following suggestions are offered in the spirit of forewarning VCP designers about issues, challenges, and controversies that they are likely to confront in designing most, if not all, VCPs. But providing specific recommendations about complete designs or key features of high-quality designs seems unrealistic. For instance, the best design decisions—and the appropriateness of particular designs—can differ greatly depending on VCP-specific circumstances, such as the wishes of taxpayers or donors, the number of victims, the nature and severity of injuries, and the VCP budget.

Early Selection of Value Judgments

The design of a VCP and how well it is implemented determine the extent of fairness, speed of compensation, and size of transaction costs. How well a VCP's design balances these three major outcomes depends on key value judgments, such as what fairness entails—for example, the relative importance of need, deservingness, and horizontal equity—and the acceptable trade-offs among the three outcomes. These value judgments provide the most promising guidance for gauging the desirability of design choices, and such guidance will be needed time and again as design decisions are made. Thus, as hard as this is, it seems best—for reasons discussed presently—for designers to choose their value judgments early, articulate them, and apply them consistently as the life of a VCP plays out.

It seems worthwhile for designers to make these decisions on fairness aspects as soon as is practical—albeit in necessarily rough terms. There are at least three major advantages of doing so. First, it saves designer time and effort—and aids efficient decisionmaking—by helping to avoid repeated reconsideration of the same issues. Second, having a clear sense of what fairness requires—*there is no correct answer*—can provide useful (albeit rough) guidance to help avoid inconsistencies about the meaning of fairness *for that VCP*, and, in turn, help designers stay faithful to their chosen principles. Third, having established principles and applying them consistently helps designers justify their decisions and enhance the legitimacy of the VCP in the eyes of victims and funders.

Similarly, it seems worthwhile for designers to decide as soon as is practical their views on the relative importance of being fair, ensuring timely compensation, and limiting transaction costs. As just discussed, doing so also should save designers time and effort, avoid inconsistencies, and enhance perceived legitimacy.

In sum, once the key value judgments are made, designers are better positioned to make the numerous major and minor design decisions.

On the Road to Best Practices

As explained, best practices for VCP designers that will command (even nearly) universal respect cannot be developed. Thus, this section emphasizes ways to improve an outcome—such as the extent of fairness, speed of compensation, and size of transaction costs—with fairly small sacrifices in other outcomes. These suggestions for VCP designers are as follows:

1. Focus on the well-being of the victims of the disaster and on meeting obligations to funders and upstream VCP creators (if any) who delegate decisions to you. For example, do not concern yourself with the potential effects of your decisions on future rates of insurance uptake or self-protection efforts. You do not

have obligations to victims of future disasters or designers of future VCPs. Moreover, the available evidence suggests that theoretical effects of your decisions on insurance uptake and physical self-protection are likely not to apply in the real world.

2. Recognize that eligibility decisions—which may often precede many other design decisions—are crucial. For this reason, think especially hard about eligibility rules. Your views about what is fair should provide useful guidance.

3. Take fraud seriously and make extensive efforts to deter it— *in relatively low-cost ways.* In many instances, highly publicized arrests and severe punishment for a fairly small number of people may be as effective as or more effective than intensive auditing of large numbers of claims, which can be expensive and create delays. There have been highly publicized arrests of people who attempted to defraud the One Fund Boston, the GCCF, and the Indiana State Fair VCP; do what you can to increase the visibility of such arrests.

4. Be aware that assigning equal payments for all fatalities—a strategy that is inconsistent with tort principles—seems less controversial than offering unequal payments; many object on moral grounds to the idea that some lives are more valuable than others.[1] For example, Feinberg—who was required to use tort principles in designing the 9/11 VCF of 2001 and, as a result, settled on widely ranging compensation levels for fatalities— has expressed substantial uneasiness with paying different amounts for each deceased victim. For example, he expressed sympathy—and, seemingly, support—for "the argument that all lives should be valued the same, regardless of status or station" (Feinberg, 2012, p. 63).

5. Be aware that—in contrast to the situation pertaining to fatalities—assigning different payments for different kinds of injuries and for injuries of differing severity seems to be widely accepted. Such variation characterized all 11 VCPs discussed in

---

[1]   As in tort, compensation to survivors of those who are killed in a catastrophe might reflect lost income or companionship—the value of which can differ greatly across victims.

this report, and no substantial controversy was evident from the information collected about them.

6. As much as possible, avoid using funding allocated or donated to your VCP to cover the administrative costs of the program. Rightly or wrongly, this is money to which victims are likely to feel entitled. For example, try to find businesses that are willing to cover administrative costs separately, and encourage donations of time and expertise to help victims understand the rules and processes and fill out forms; in addition, seek professional volunteers to help process claims and perform audits.

7. To mitigate delays in payments to victims, consider using interim payments to help address victims' immediate needs. Interim payments were used, for example, by the 9/11 VCF of 2001 (Feinberg, 2005, p. 45), the Tucson Together Fund, and the One Fund Boston (Fox, 2014).

8. To save on administrative costs, consider offering fairly small payments—as the sole compensation from the VCP—that are relatively easily available to victims. Presumably, such payments are attractive only to victims with relatively small losses, and, alas, those who are not truly eligible. The quick payments offered as part of the GCCF VCP seem to have this effect (in addition to mitigating delays in payments).

9. To save on administrative costs, make sure that program rules and processes are no more complex than needed to achieve other goals. For example, consider carefully whether a lack of collateral-source offsets would undermine fairness enough to warrant the resulting extra delays and administrative costs.

10. Avoid unnecessary claim and documentation burdens that are borne by victims. Making or keeping claim forms simple and understandable to victims with relatively low reading comprehension levels could help a lot. Moreover, as suggested earlier, encourage community members to donate time to help victims complete paperwork.

11. Avoid using donations that were solicited by invoking sympathy for the direct victims of the disaster to help other groups, such as community members at large. Such use of funds has

greatly annoyed those eligible for compensation from a VCP. One tactic for furthering this goal is to make sure that fundraisers are clear about how donations will be used. The One Fund Boston seems to have been effective in mitigating—but perhaps not entirely eliminating—this problem.

12. Limit the number of funds or programs providing compensation to victims—ideally, to only one. Efforts to coordinate among several compensators may well be futile, and they will almost surely increase payment delays and administrative costs. Thus, *preempting* the creation of multiple funds or programs seems more promising than effectively *coordinating* among them. The One Fund Boston seems like an excellent model in this regard, because community leaders announced its creation within one day of the incident, and it seems that the fund succeeded in attracting a very large share of all donations intended to help the bombing victims.

Concluding Remarks

VCP designers face complex tasks with no correct solutions. The designers are often monitored, criticized, second-guessed, and challenged by various stakeholders. The most experienced and prominent designer of U.S. VCPs has cautioned that "no good deed goes unpunished" (Feinberg, 2005, p. 92). This report aims to provide information, ideas, and suggestions that could help VCP designers act more quickly and achieve better outcomes for victims and other stakeholders. It is hoped that some of these suggestions will be used by VCP designers to help future victims and reduce future designers' punishments for their good deeds.

References

"$77 Million Fund Created for Reno Air Races Crash Victims," *Reno Gazette-Journal*, March 22, 2012. As of September 2, 2014:
http://www.rgj.com/story/news/2014/03/23/
77-million-fund-created-for-reno-air-races-crash-victims/6611245/

Abel, David, "Marathon Bombings Survivors Seek More Aid," *Boston Globe*, June 21, 2014. As of September 9, 2014:
http://www.bostonglobe.com/metro/2014/06/20/
marathon-bombing-survivors-question-one-fund/mbSvBh251ZrlgoG6F8YVaP/
story.html

Alcindor, Yamiche, and Oren Dorell, "Aurora Shooting Shows: After Tragedy Comes Controversy," *USA Today*, September 4, 2012.

Alexander, Janet Cooper, "Procedural Design and Terror Victim Compensation," *DePaul Law Review*, Vol. 53, No. 2, 2003.

Altimari, Dave, "Former Federal Judge to Help Decide Who Gets Sandy Hook Money, Sources Say," *Hartford Courant*, April 18, 2013. As of December 29, 2014:
http://articles.courant.com/2013-04-18/news/
hc-sandyhook-money-nevas-20130418_
1_nevas-foundation-board-kenneth-feinberg

———, "Newtown Official: Sandy Hook Shootings Donations Divided Town," *Hartford Courant*, September 12, 2014. As of September 23, 2014:
http://www.courant.com/news/connecticut/
hc-sandy-hook-commission-llodra-20140912-story.html

American Bar Association, *Rule of Law in Times of Major Disaster*, Chicago, August 2007. As of May 23, 2016:
http://www.americanbar.org/content/dam/aba/migrated/disaster/docs/
rol_in_times_of_disasters.authcheckdam.pdf

Andersen, Travis, "N.J. Woman Accused of Trying to Scam One Fund Boston," *Boston Globe*, August 9, 2013. As of December 28, 2014:
http://www.bostonglobe.com/metro/2013/08/09/woman-accused-trying-scam-one-fund-boston/DpEproZSlOX7Lz1Y3cKsWO/story.html

Annear, Steve, "Boston Man Arrested for Filing Fraudulent Request for One Fund Money," *Boston Magazine*, July 2, 2013. As of December 28, 2014:
http://www.bostonmagazine.com/news/blog/2013/07/02/one-fund-fraud-claim-branden-mattier/

Applebome, Peter, "Foundation to Distribute $4 Million to Families Affected by Newtown Massacre," *New York Times*, April 10, 2013, p. A19. As of December 28, 2014:
http://www.nytimes.com/2013/04/11/nyregion/foundation-to-distribute-4-million-to-families-affected-by-newtown-massacre.html

Associated Press, "Newtown Struggling to Divvy Up Donations for Sandy Hook Shooting Victims," *Insurance Journal*, July 2, 2013a. As of January 19, 2014:
http://www.insurancejournal.com/news/east/2013/07/02/297391.htm

———, "Plan Endorsed for Sandy Hook Community Foundation Distributions," *Newtown Bee*, July 17, 2013b. As of May 23, 2016:
http://newtownbee.com/plan-endorsed-for-sandy-hook-community-foundation-distributions/

———, "Court Upholds $5M Cap in Indiana Stage Collapse Case," *Chicago Tribune*, January 14, 2015. As of June 10, 2015:
http://www.chicagotribune.com/news/nationworld/chi-indiana-stage-collapse-20150114-story.html

Barnett, Kyle, "Sentences Handed Out for Fraudulent Claims Stemming from 2010 BP Oil Spill," *Louisiana Record*, August 12, 2010. As of December 28, 2014:
http://louisianarecord.com/news/254077-sentences-handed-out-for-fraudulent-claims-stemming-from-2010-bp-oil-spill

Bea, Keith, *Federal Stafford Act Disaster Assistance: Presidential Declarations, Eligible Activities, and Funding*, Washington, D.C.: Congressional Research Service, RL33053, March 16, 2010.

Berkowitz, Elizabeth, "The Problematic Role of the Special Master: Undermining the Legitimacy of the September 11th Victim Compensation Fund," *Yale Law & Policy Review*, Vol. 24, No. 1, 2006.

Bernstein, Lenny, "Boston Marathon Bombing Victims Will Split $61 Million," *Washington Post*, June 29, 2013a. As of December 28, 2014:
http://www.washingtonpost.com/national/health-science/boston-marathon-bombing-victims-will-split-61-million/2013/06/28/a8114090-e010-11e2-b2d4-ea6d8f477a01_story.html?Post+generic=%3Ftid%3Dsm_twitter_washingtonpost

————, "For Some Boston Marathon Bombing Victims, Charity Checks Bring Frustration," *Washington Post*, September 15, 2013b. As of December 28, 2014: http://www.washingtonpost.com/national/health-science/ for-some-boston-marathon-bombing-victims-charity-checks-bring-frustration/ 2013/09/15/759bd786-1983-11e3-82ef-a059e54c49d0_story.html

————, "Victim Critical of Marathon Fund," *Valley News*, October 3, 2013c.

Birnbaum, Sheila L., *Second Annual Status Report: September 11th Victim Compensation Fund*, Washington, D.C.: September 11th Victim Compensation Fund, November 2013.

Bronstad, Amanda, "GM Fund Closes, Suits Still Pile Up," *National Law Journal*, April 16, 2015. As of May 28, 2015: http://www.nationallawjournal.com/id=1202723757468/ GM-Fund-Closes-Suits-Still-Pile-Up

Brumfeld, Ben, "Payments from Aurora Victim Relief Fund Finalized," CNN, November 18, 2012. As of January 19, 2014: http://www.cnn.com/2012/11/17/us/colorado-aurora-compensation/

Burbank, Kent, "A Training Outline—Tucson's Experience in Managing Multiple Victim Funds after the January 8th Tucson Tragedy," Tucson, Ariz., Pima County Attorney's Office, Victim Services Division, undated. As of May 23, 2016: https://www.ncjtc.org/CONF/Ovcconf/AttMat/ Understanding%20Victim%20Compensation_Burbank_Handout.pdf

Campbell, Alex, "$13.2M Settlement Stalls in Indian Stage Collapse," *Indianapolis Star*, August 16, 2012. As of September 5, 2014: http://usatoday30.usatoday.com/news/nation/story/2012-08-16/ indiana-stage-collapse/57091226/1

Christoffersen, John, "Newtown Donations: Panel Suggests Breakdown of $7.7 Million Between Families," Associated Press, July 11, 2013. As of May 23, 2016: http://www.cbsnews.com/news/ panel-suggests-77m-breakdown-of-newtown-payments/

Citizens Property Insurance Corporation, "Company Overview," web page, 2014, no longer available.

City of Revere, "Revere Tornado Relief Fund Administrator Announces Distribution of a Quarter of a Million Dollars to Be Made to 150 Eligible Applicants," December 8, 2014. As of May 29, 2015: http://www.revere.org/news/post/ revere-tornado-relief-fund-administrator-announces-distribution-of-a-quarter-of-a-million-dollars-to-be-made-to-150-eligible-applicants

CNN Wire Staff, "2 Charged with Filing Claims to Get Indiana State Fair Stage Collapse Money," CNN, December 28, 2011. As of September 9, 2014: http://www.cnn.com/2011/12/28/justice/indiana-fair-claims/

Colorado Organization for Victim Assistance, "What We Do," web page, undated. As of September 23, 2014: http://www.coloradocrimevictims.org/about-cova.html

Conk, George W., "Diving into the Wreck: BP and Kenneth Feinberg's Gulf Coast Gambit," *Roger Williams University Law Review*, Vol. 17, No. 137, 2012, pp. 137–183.

Conrad, David R., and Edward A. Thomas, "Proposal 2: Reforming Federal Support for Risky Development," in Michael Greenstone, Max Harris, Karen Li, Adam Looney, and Jeremy Patashnik, eds., *15 Ways to Rethink the Federal Budget*, Washington, D.C.: Brookings Institution, February 2013, pp. 17–22.

Dauber, Michele Landis, "The War of 1812, September 11th, and the Politics of Compensation, *DePaul Law Review*, Vol. 53, No. 2, 2003.

Deam, Jenny, "Colorado Shooting Victims Still Waiting to See Donations," *Los Angeles Times*, September 16, 2012a. As of December 28, 2014: http://articles.latimes.com/2012/sep/16/nation/la-na-aurora-massacre-20120916

———, "Aurora Massacre: Funds to Reach Theater Victims Next Month," *Los Angeles Times*, October 15, 2012b. As of December 28, 2014: http://articles.latimes.com/2012/oct/15/nation/la-na-nn-aurora-victim-fund-distribution-20121015

———, "Charity Funds for Tragedy Victims Getting Trickier," *Los Angeles Times*, June 1, 2013. As of January 19, 2014: http://articles.latimes.com/2013/jun/01/nation/la-na-victim-funds-20130602

Diller, Matthew, "Tort and Social Welfare Principles in the Victim Compensation Fund," *DePaul Law Review*, Vol. 53, No. 2, 2003, pp. 719–768.

Disis, Jill, "Stage Collapse Victim Asks Appeals Court to Throw Out State's Liability Cap," *Indianapolis Star*, December 16, 2014. As of June 10, 2015: http://www.whas11.com/story/news/local/indiana/2014/12/16/indiana-state-fair-stage-collapse/20470423/

Dixon, Lloyd, Noreen Clancy, Seth A. Seabury, and Adrian Overton, *The National Flood Insurance Program's Market Penetration Rate: Estimates and Policy Implications*, Santa Monica, Calif.: RAND Corporation, TR-300-FEMA, 2006. As of May 23, 2016: http://www.rand.org/pubs/technical_reports/TR300.html

Dixon, Lloyd, and Rachel Kaganoff Stern, *Compensation for Losses from the 9/11 Attacks*, Santa Monica, Calif.: RAND Corporation, MG-264-ICJ, 2004. As of May 23, 2016: http://www.rand.org/pubs/monographs/MG264.html

Epstein, Richard A., "Catastrophic Responses to Catastrophic Risks," *Journal of Risk and Uncertainty*, Vol. 12, 1996, pp. 287–308.

Faure, Michael G., "Financial Compensation for Victims of Catastrophes: A Law and Economics Perspective," *Law & Policy*, Vol. 29, No. 3, July 2007, pp. 339–367.

Faure, Michael, and Ton Hartlief, eds., *Financial Compensation for Victims of Catastrophe: A Comparative Legal Approach*, New York: Springer-Verlag/Wien, 2006.

Feinberg, Kenneth R., *What Is Life Worth?* New York: Public Affairs, 2005.

———, "The September 11th Victim Compensation Fund of 2001: Policy and Precedent," *New York Law School Law Review*, Vol. 56, 2011/2012, pp. 1115–1118.

———, *Who Gets What? Fair Compensation After Tragedy and Financial Upheaval*, New York: Public Affairs, 2012.

Feinberg, Kenneth, Camille S. Biros, Jordana Harris Feldman, Deborah E. Greenspan, and Jacqueline E. Zins, *Final Report of the Special Master for the September 11th Victim Compensation Fund of 2001*, Vol. 2, 2004. As of May 23, 2016:
http://www.coherentbabble.com/signingstatements/DOJ/DOJfinal_report[1]911-Comp.pdf

Findley, Michelle L., "Statutory Tort Caps: What States Should Do When Available Funds Seem Inadequate," *Indiana Law Review*, Vol. 46, No. 3, 2013.

Fox, Jeremy C., "One Fund Boston Plans Second Distribution, of $12 Million, to Bombing Survivors, Families in July," *Boston Globe*, January 2, 2104. As of December 28, 2014:
http://www.bostonglobe.com/metro/2014/01/02/one-fund-boston-plans-second-distribution-million-bombing-survivors-families-july/jZOSKIHIIzrR2VQ0bcsuVK/story.html

Garber, Steven, *Economic Effects of Product Liability and Other Litigation Involving the Safety and Effectiveness of Pharmaceuticals*, Santa Monica, Calif.: RAND Corporation, MG-1259-ICJ, 2013. As of May 23, 2016:
http://www.rand.org/pubs/monographs/MG1259.html

Harrington, Scott E., "Rethinking Disaster Policy," *Regulation*, Vol. 23, No. 1, 2000, pp. 40–46.

Henson, Shannon, "Minn. Reaches Deals With Bridge Collapse Victims," *Law360*, April 16, 2009. As of December 28, 2014:
http://www.law360.com/articles/97244/minn-reaches-deals-with-bridge-collapse-victims

Indiana State Fair Commission, "Indiana State Fair Relief Fund—Final Protocol," undated. As of May 23, 2016:
http://www.thefederation.org/documents/05.Protocol%20%20FINAL-Clean.pdf

————, "State Fair Commission Takes Steps to Distribute Remembrance Fund Donations," news release, August 31, 2011. As of May 23, 2016: https://secure.in.gov/sfc/files/State_Fair_Commission_takes_steps_to_distribute_Remembrance_Fund_donations.pdf

Jametti, Mario, and Thomas von Ungern-Sternberg, "Hurricane Insurance in Florida," Center for Economic Studies and Ifo Institute (CESifo) Munich, unpublished manuscript, August 2011.

Kuppa-Apte, Pallavi, "Feinberg Discusses Fund Distribution," *The Dartmouth*, May 11, 2011. As of June 3, 2016: http://thedartmouth.com/2011/05/11/feinberg-discusses-fund-distribution/

Kusisto, Laura, "New Milestone in Post-Sandy Housing Recovery," *Wall Street Journal*, September 1, 2014. As of September 11, 2014: http://online.wsj.com/articles/new-milestone-in-post-sandy-housing-recovery-1409622283

Landers, Elizabeth, "Woman Arrested in Alleged Half-Million-Dollar Scam of Boston Victims' Fund," CNN, July 19, 2013. As of December 28, 2014: http://www.cnn.com/2013/07/19/justice/massachusetts-boston-fund-allegations/

Landis, Michelle L., ""Let Me Next Time Be 'Tried by Fire'": Disaster Relief and the Origins of the American Welfare State 1789–1874," *Northwestern University Law Review*, Vol. 92, No. 3, 1998, pp. 967–1034.

"Last of State Fair Relief Fund Distributed to Victims Monday," *Daily Pilot*, November 21, 2011, no longer available.

LaTourette, Tom, James N. Dertouzos, Christina E. Steiner, and Noreen Clancy, *Earthquake Insurance and Disaster Assistance: The Effect of Catastrophe Obligation Guarantees on Federal Disaster-Assistance Expenditures in California*, Santa Monica, Calif.: RAND Corporation, TR-896-CEA, 2010. As of May 23, 2016: http://www.rand.org/pubs/technical_reports/TR896.html

Ly, Laura, "Newtown Victim Families Could Each Receive $281,000 from Donated Funds," CNN, July 13, 2013. As of December 29, 2014: http://www.cnn.com/2013/07/12/us/newtown-donations/

McDonell, Colin, "The Gulf Coast Claims Facility and the Deepwater Horizon Litigation: Judicial Regulation of Private Compensation Schemes," *Stanford Law Review*, Vol. 64, No. 3, March 2012, p. 765.

Minneapolis Foundation, *Minnesota Helps—Bridge Disaster Fund, Report to the Community*, September 2009.

Mullenix, Linda S., "Prometheus Unbound: The Gulf Coast Claims Facility as a Means for Resolving Mass Tort Claims—A Fund Too Far," *Louisiana Law Review*, Vol. 71, No. 3, Spring 2011, pp. 819–916.

————, "Designing Compensatory Funds: In Search of First Principles," University of Texas School of Law, Public Law and Legal Theory Research Paper Series, No. 567, 2014.

Mullenix, Linda S., and Kristen B. Stewart, "The September 11th Victim Compensation Fund: Fund Approaches to Resolving Mass Litigation," *Connecticut Insurance Law Journal*, Vol. 9, 2002–2003, pp. 121–152.

Nagareda, Richard A., *Mass Torts in a World of Settlements*, Chicago: University of Chicago Press, 2007.

Napa Valley Vintners, "Neighbors Helping Neighbors—Napa Valley Presses on After Earthquake," web page, undated. As of May 29, 2015: http://www.napavintners.com/earthquake/

National Conference of State Legislatures, "State Sovereign Immunity and Tort Liability," September 8, 2010. As of September 23, 2014: http://www.ncsl.org/research/transportation/ state-sovereign-immunity-and-tort-liability.aspx

Newtown–Sandy Hook Community Foundation, "Newtown–Sandy Hook Victim Compensation Fund: Final Protocol," July 17, 2013. As of May 23, 2016: http://www.nshcf.org/wp-content/uploads/2013/07/NSHCF-final-protocal.pdf

Office of the Indiana Attorney General, "Attorney General Zoeller: Feinberg's Victim Compensation Advice a Model for the Future," press release, September 11, 2012.

————, "Attorney General Zoeller: Indiana Wins Key Legal Victory in State Fair Litigation," press release, March 11, 2014.

Parry, Wayne, "NJ Wants Sandy Money Shifted to Housing Repairs," Associated Press, November 6, 2013. As of December 28, 2014: http://www.northjersey.com/news/ nj-state-news/n-j-wants-sandy-money-shifted-to-housing-repairs-1.571221

Partlett, David F., and Russell L. Weaver, "BP Oil Spill: Compensation, Agency Costs, and Restitution," *Washington & Lee Law Review*, Vol. 68, No. 3, 2011, pp. 1341–1375.

Peck, Robert S., "The Victims Compensation Fund: Born from a Unique Confluence of Events Not Likely to Be Duplicated," *DePaul Law Review*, Vol. 53, No. 2, 2003, pp. 209–230.

Priest, George L., "The Problematic Structure of the September 11th Victim Compensation Fund," *DePaul Law Review*, Vol. 53, No. 2, 2003, pp. 527–545.

Rabin, Robert L., "The Quest for Fairness in Compensating Victims of September 11," *Cleveland State Law Review*, Vol. 49, No. 4, 2001, pp. 573–589.

Rabin, Robert L., and Suzanne A. Bratis, "United States," in Michael Faure and Tom Hartlief, eds., *Financial Compensation for Victims of Catastrophes: A Comparative Legal Approach*, 2006, pp. 303–359.

Rabin, Robert L., and Stephen D. Sugarman, "The Case for Specially Compensating the Victims of Terrorist Acts: An Assessment," *Hofstra Law Review*, Vol. 35, No. 3, Spring 2007, pp. 901–915.

Reno Air Racing Association Accident Compensation Fund Program, "Protocol," web page, undated, no longer available to the public.

September 11th Victim Compensation Fund, "Frequently Asked Questions," web page, undated. As of February 25, 2016:
http://www.vcf.gov/faq.html

———, *VCF Program Statistics*, September 6, 2015. As of February 25, 2016:
http://www.vcf.gov/pdf/VCFProgramStatistics09092015.pdf

Stafford, Dave, "AG: State Fair Stage Collapse Victim Payments Completed," *Indiana Lawyer*, December 20, 2012. As of September 5, 2014:
http://www.theindianalawyer.com/
ag-state-fair-stage-collapse-victim-payments-completed/PARAMS/article/30384

———, "State Fair Stage Collapse Appeal Puts Tort Caps on Trial," *Indiana Lawyer*, December 31, 2014. As of June 10, 2015:
http://www.theindianalawyer.com/
state-fair-stage-collapse-appeal-puts-tort-caps-on-trial/PARAMS/article/35999

State of Connecticut, Department of Consumer Protection, Office of the Attorney General, "Attorney General, Consumer Protection Post Information from Sandy Hook-Related Charities," web page, April 16, 2013. As of September 23, 2014:
http://www.ct.gov/ag/cwp/view.asp?Q=522908&A=2341

Steenson, Mike, and Joseph Michael Sayler, "The Legacy of the 9/11 Fund and the Minnesota Bridge Collapse Fund; Creating a Template for Compensating Victims of Future Mass-Tort Catastrophes," *William Mitchell Law Review*, Vol. 35, No. 2, 2009.

Stewart, Larry S., Danile L. Cohen, and Karen L. Marangi, "The September 11th Victim Compensation Fund: Past or Prologue? *Connecticut Insurance Law Journal*, Vol. 9, 2002–2003, pp. 153–178.

"Stronger Than the Storm—Hurricane Sandy One Year On," *The Economist*, October 19, 2013, p. 36. As of December 28, 2014:
http://www.highbeam.com/doc/1G1-345848271.html

Sugarman, Stephen D., "Roles of Government in Compensating Disaster Victims," *Issues in Legal Scholarship*, Vol. 6, No. 3, 2007.

Trial Lawyers Care, "About Trial Lawyers Care," web page, undated. As of September 10, 2014:
http://www.triallawyerscare.org/about-trial-lawyers-care/

"UConn Scholarship Fund for Sandy Hook Survivors Raises $1M," *NBC Connecticut*, March 20, 2013. As of December 28, 2014:
http://www.nbcconnecticut.com/news/local/
UConn-Scholarship-Fund-for-Sandy-Hook-Survivors-Raises-1M-199170121.html

U.S. Department of Justice, "Final Rule: James Zadroga 9/11 Health and Compensation Act of 2010," *Federal Register* 76, No. 169, August 31, 2011, pp. 54112–54126. As of September 4, 2014:
https://www.gpo.gov/fdsys/pkg/FR-2011-08-31/pdf/2011-22295.pdf

Virginia Tech, Office of University Relations, "Virginia Tech Distributes Hokie Spirit Monies to Families of Those Slain on April 16 and to Selected Others," October 30, 2007. As of September 23, 2014:
http://www.vtnews.vt.edu/articles/2007/10/2007-645.html

Weizel, Richard, "Newtown Donations Created Deep Rift After Shootings, Official Says," Reuters, September 12, 2014. As of December 29, 2014:
http://www.businessinsider.com/
r-newtown-donations-created-deep-rift-after-shootings-official-says-2014-9

Wharton Risk Management and Decision Processes Center, *Managing Large-Scale Risks in a New Era of Catastrophes: Insuring, Mitigating and Financing Recovery from Natural Disasters in the United States*, Philadelphia, Pa., March 2008.